PET
SEX

Other books by Peter Neville

DO CATS NEED SHRINKS?
DO DOGS NEED SHRINKS?
CLAWS AND PURRS

Help for pets with behaviour problems

THE ASSOCIATION OF PET BEHAVIOUR COUNSELLORS

The APBC comprises many professional members throughout the United Kingdom and overseas who treat behaviour problems in pets exclusively on referral from veterinary surgeons. So if your pet has a behaviour problem, sexual or otherwise, a member of the APBC may be able to help you with a detailed personal consultation. Please ask your veterinary surgeon for details of the nearest APBC member's practice or write to:

The Honorary Secretary, APBC,
257 Royal College Street, London NW1 9LU, England.

PETER NEVILLE

PET SEX

SIDGWICK & JACKSON
LONDON

First published 1993 by Sidgwick & Jackson Limited
a division of Pan Macmillan Publishers Limited
Cavaye Place London SW10 9PG
and Basingstoke

Associated companies throughout the world

ISBN 0 283 06149 9

1 3 5 7 9 8 6 4 2

A CIP catalogue record for this book is available from the British Library

Typeset by the Bessant Neville Partnership, Salisbury, Wilts
Printed by Mackays of Chatham plc

Contents

For Claire and Sinead, my favourite girls, and for my dad, John. And to Cass our Bullmastiff, Scud our English Bull Terrier cross Border Collie, our cats Bullet, Bean, Flirty Bottom and Peru, our nine ducks and nine goldfish for having the decency to control their sexuality and behave as every pet behaviourist's own pets surely should do!

Acknowledgements

I would like to thank my wife Claire for keeping the text of this book within the realms of human decency (just). Claire, together with Clare Tickner, our much appreciated secretary, has put up admirably with my responding to the irresistible temptations of the subject matter with occasional outbursts of my smutty school boy sense of humour during the writing of this book. I'm getting better through understanding, patience and tolerance . . . ! Many thanks also to my sister-in-law, Karen Bessant, for all her hard work in compiling the physiological research for this book and to Helen Gummer, my editor, for her professionalism and inscrutable, unflappable coolness in the face of the contents. A true 'sexpert'! Wit and great friend Russell Jones should be locked away for his cartoons, but I'll remember to thank him beforehand for his excellent works in this book. And finally thanks to all my clients over the years who have told me about their pets' sexual behaviour — either for their sense of humour or for their courage in overcoming their acute embarrassment — if you hadn't 'come out' with your pets' sexual indiscretions and confused reactions, our understanding of the sexuality of our pets would have been restricted to the closet. Thank you, your anonymity and that of your pets is guaranteed!

Foreplay

'If sex ever rears its ugly head, close your eyes before you see the rest of it' ALAN AYCKBOURN

It had been an excellent first course but finally she just had to approach the subject. 'I hope you don't mind me asking . . .' was all she needed to say, and I knew I was on duty again. Eventually just about everyone I meet has to ask me something about the mad cat, dog or other pet that they own or used to own as a child or which is kept anonymously (ahem) by a long-suffering friend. Of course I don't mind. After all, if you put your head over the parapet, it's inevitable that people will want to take a shot or two at you, especially with a subject as popular and amusing as the behaviour of our pets and as free of politics and religion for lunch and dinner conversations. I always feel grateful that as a pet shrink most of the stories I hear are interesting and often funny. If nothing else, they certainly help to break the ice with people I've never met before. I'm just glad that I'm not a human doctor or psychologist having to listen to tales of woe of a human kind which would be much more awkward to offer help about and certainly more difficult to laugh at.

'It's just that I have a dog, and he's really sweet and friendly, but he will keep . . . well, you know, making amorous advances towards me. My husband just thinks it's funny but, well, I wondered if there's anything I can do about it.'

Ahah. Maybe this won't be so bad. Usually I get the feline house-training questions at the very moment the Bernaise sauce gets delivered, or have to endure tales of diet-related aggression in dogs just as I'm about to savage a huge steak and have to talk about offering the poor dog blander meals. But sex! This gives me the chance to seize the embarrassment of the moment and gain some revenge for another meal spent consulting. 'What exactly does he do?' I counter, waiting for the juicy details that I'm sure will bring the colour to the good lady's cheeks. In a low voice, she explains that in the evening when the family is gathered on the comfy chairs watching television in the living room, Piers the dog will grab her leg, so provocatively and invitingly crossed over, and with a vice-like grip attempt to make mad, passionate love to it. Worse than this, he's had several leaps at her as she's got out of bed or stepped out from the shower and is much more vulnerable.

'I hope you've had his nails trimmed,' I throw in casually, in a vain effort to keep the conversation as flippant as possible, but it's too late. Having crossed the bridge and broached the unmentionable subject, we're into the full serious nature of it all and the urgent request for advice. Oh well, it could still be fun, and I launch into the professional pet psychologist's preliminary questions concerning the age, history, lifestyle and general character of Piers, whom, we have already clearly established, is a male dog. About to furnish my suffering dining companion with up-to-the-minute information about the secondary sexual development, hormonal surges and changing social behaviour during the adolescence of the male dog, I found myself interrupted by the lone diner on the next table.

'You must be mad,' said the middle-aged lady authoritatively, staring somewhere over our heads and past the waitress caught in the cross fire with her side salad. 'Cut his balls off immediately, and if that doesn't work, try his head and get another dog . . . and make it a bitch next time. I've never had trouble with my dogs because I've never kept males. They all think with their balls, whether it's dogs or men, and if we cut them all off, the world would be a lot less troublesome. Look at that Saddam Hussein, power-mad maniac . . .' she rattled on, but I'd already switched off, remembering all those horrid hardcase Rottweilers and German Shepherd Dogs called 'Saddam' that I'd treated a few months after the Gulf war. I surfaced to see my lady companion looking aghast at our neighbour. She turned back towards me and, in a slightly lower tone than before, enquired, 'Is that really what Piers needs? That's what my vet suggested, and I don't mind having it done, providing it's going to work.'

'Poor love,' interjected the waitress, risking her tip with the middle-aged lady but having already made up her mind that there probably wasn't much to risk with someone of such hard-hearted opinions. 'All he probably needs is a little attention and a friend to play with. You can't go de-sexing him just because he gets a bit excited occasionally. That's a terrible thing to do to your little doggie, he'd never forgive you.'

My companion looked at me with a face that said she was now utterly embarrassed and totally confused. The whole world had joined in on her private conversation with her captive pet shrink, brought the entire problem down to a simple question of what to do with Piers' bits and then given her contradictory advice. I smiled knowingly and suggested, in a loud enough voice for the waitress and the battleaxe to hear, that the treatment of all behavioural problems in pets, especially those of such a delicate personal nature, is best considered through an in-depth consultation and that perhaps she and I should meet at her house to decide what might be the best option for Piers' little problem. Wishing she'd never raised the subject in the first place, she smiled, and more so when I added that we would try to avoid having Piers castrated if at all possible as matters were rarely so simple as to have a solution in the unkindest cut of all.

I sliced into my steak in a symbolic kind of way but didn't really taste much of my lunch, nor did I take much notice of the rest of our conversation, which was kept to totally unprovocative and mundane tittle-tattle to avoid further unwanted opinions being thrown in from the table on our right. But as I chewed and chatted, my subconscious was working overtime, wondering how it was that two parts of a dog's anatomy or, more accurately, his unwanted sexual attentions, could inspire such a gamut of human emotions and opinions and cause the breaking of the unwritten law of British social etiquette that you keep yourself to yourself. There was my typical client: the sensible and caring owner, seeking some sensible advice about her dog's behaviour, despite the delicate nature of Piers' antics. And then we had the anti-male harridan applying her own forthright human values to a dog: his problems, like the rest of the world's that concerned the feeble-minded testosterone-led male, could be tackled with a simple cure-all. There'd be no fuss and no consideration of the owner's attachment to her dog or the likely effectiveness of her cutting suggestions. Then there was the highly sympathetic but crushingly anthropomorphic waitress who viewed Piers as a little human rather than a dog. She could no more consider castrating him than she would her boyfriend if he got a little over-amorous after a night out. And yet the focus of the whole uncomfortable exchange of views was Piers the dog, doing what came naturally for him. Though his behaviour was, in human terms, thoroughly reprehensible, at least he bore none of the ignorant malicious intent, or over-emotional misguided attitudes of the two outsiders who had felt the need to discuss the fate of his genitals. The owner and I could at least consider ourselves as possessing a sense of empathy and realism about Piers and his problems, and my job as a specialist would be to assess exactly what type of treatment could best maintain the joy of her overall relationship with her pet.

But I fell to wondering just what it was about sex and the single dog that could produce such a situation. Why was it that Piers' owner should have tolerated her dog's behaviour even this far? And just how did I come to be sitting in the middle of this conversation about a dog's sex life? The subject was so easily raised, and created a maelstrom of human emotion, yet when the sex life of a human member of the family becomes aberrant or invasive the subject is so often taboo. And that's really where this book about sex and our pets was conceived, if that is the word. I decided to look at how we tolerate, suffer from, understand, fail to understand, treat and react to sex in our pets using some of the many sad and hilarious cases of sexual problems both normal and decidedly bizarre that I've encountered in my career. The vast majority of pet owners whose pets I have seen professionally over the years have been easy-going, sensible and well-balanced folk, save only for many of those cases which have concerned the sexual antics of their cats, dogs or rabbits. Then my client base divides nicely into two groups: first the highly amused who are great fun to get to know because they invariably share the same sense of humour as me, and though they want their pet's problems sorted out are enjoying the hilarity of telling everyone about it all. Take, for instance, the surely unique case of Jasper.

The cat and the radiator — a tale of hot passion!

Dear Mr Neville

Our year-old cat Jasper seems to have fallen in love with the radiator in our front room since we turned the heating on for the winter. Even though he is a neutered male, every so often he gets a wild look in his eye and rushes up to what we presume he thinks is his girl-friend. He somehow manages to get a hold on either side of the radiator with his front paws and legs and then proceeds to mount her as fast as he can, while making the most amazing screeching and high-pitched grunting noises. At first we thought this was hilarious, but now we're actually quite worried about Jasper, even though he's never done himself any harm. Each love-making session lasts a matter of a minute or so, and usually ends with Jasper losing his grip, falling off and then dashing out into the garden, perhaps to tell his mates all about his latest conquest. Please do you have any explanation for Jasper's behaviour? It's only the one radiator that he loves and he simply curls asleep next to the others like any normal cat. Is there anything we can do to help him, like get him a female cat?

Yours sincerely

Gillian and David Thomas

Well, this I just had to go and see! And I wasn't disappointed, for unlike many feline behaviour cases that I treat, Jasper did actually demonstrate the problem in question there and then in front of me. I must be honest and say that I nearly died laughing, but at the same time felt rather sorry for the clearly disturbed but otherwise normal and friendly Jasper. I reached into the science section of my brain for some kind of 'professional' explanation to offer the Thomas family, who were still laughing. Clearly, for them, curing the problem was not of paramount importance and, providing Jasper wasn't actually suffering in his affair with the radiator, his behaviour was still a great source of amusement and a superb party trick for them to impress their guests with.

'While the process of courtship in cats, especially sexual displays by the female, will encourage any willing male to show interest, it is her scent that tells him when she is ready and willing to be mated,' I droned.

The sniggers continued and, as I didn't have a clue what else to suggest — after all, you can't castrate a tom cat twice — I carried on regardless. 'That scent alone sniffed on the wind or in a recently deposited urine mark can make a tom cat very excited, even without the female being in front of him. And while that excitement brings its most marked response in a mature, experienced, uncastrated tom cat, no little reaction can often be observed in young males who were castrated before they even met a female cat. Such is the primeval need to procreate that even the inexperienced can be turned on by the appropriate signals, a trigger system that lies deep within the cat's brain, and not exclusively in the two bits that were removed when Jasper was castrated.'

Then, from the waffle, the almost plausible theory arrived from deep in my brain: perhaps it was a similar scent to that of a female cat on heat that wafted from some organic jointing compound in the radiator and its pipework that inspired poor confused Jasper to mount something so bizarre so enthusiastically. Who knows? But certainly, whenever the radiator reached a critical temperature,

Jasper followed suit and locked it in his passionate embrace.

It seemed good enough and I left, promising to contact my learned colleagues and consult lots of books in search of any other theories that might lead us to an explanation and suggest a course of treatment. But it wasn't necessary. Like all passing fancies of the heart, Jasper's obsession stopped one day a few months after my visit, but for what reason I could again only make a wild guess at. Perhaps he found a new love in the shape of that seductive washing machine in the kitchen, or even finally directed his attentions to the more normal allure of his friend, the female tabby who lived with the Jenkins family down the road.

Or just maybe my original theory was right and, because spring had arrived, the love of his life had turned off and gone permanently cold on him. But whatever the reason for Jasper's cure, his was one of those nice self-resolving cases that precluded me having to undertake too much further study into the feline mind to design a plan for treatment. But then again, perhaps when the cold weather returns, Jasper's affections for his favourite radiator will surge again and I'll be getting another phone call!

Wild hunches apart, an explanation of how and why cats and dogs function sexually or socio-sexually alone can often help relieve the stress for the owner of living with what can amount to a canine sex-fiend or feline pervert. Reminding owners that dogs are dogs and cats are cats first, and human companion animals second, and explaining a little about how we relate to each other across the species divide helps to remove any feelings of disgust and rejection on the owner's part when normal and sensible communication between the two has broken down.

But then there's my second group of clients, the seriously and often sadly confused owners. Though they are very rare in my casebooks, the combination of their

pet's sexual antics and their tolerance, or even encouragement, of them has seriously confused their relationship to their mutual denigration. If treating the pet under such circumstances can be difficult, trying to get the owner to seek psychological help of a human kind is downright impossible.

Listen carefully for a sexual perversion

The case of Robbie the Jack Russell puts my dining companion's tale about her dog's sexual advances in the shade. She at least was an unwilling participant. Robbie's owner, Roger Arthur, a respectable professional man in his late forties, contacted me by telephone one evening about four years ago with an enquiry that went something like this: 'Hello, Mr Neville. I wonder if you can help me. I trust that this is in confidence for reasons which may become clear to you'.' Yes, of course,' I said, and his secret has been kept . . . until now (though names and locations are changed to protect the reputation of both parties). 'I have an eighteen month old Jack Russell dog, a male called Robbie, who has been my sole companion since my wife and I divorced a year ago. I take him everywhere with me, even to my office, and he sleeps on my bed at night, unless it's cold, in which case, he sleeps in it. He wants for nothing, is friendly and playful and, frankly, he's less trouble than my family and a darn sight more fun.'

'Ah, perhaps a bitter one here,' I surmised, and started to think how straightforward the relationship we enjoy with our dogs is in most cases. We love, protect and care for them with as much effort as we want to make and they make minimal demands on us emotionally and financially. They're usually closely bonded to us even if we're not very good owners and they want to be with us because they view us as part of their pack, as other dogs in fact. But after emotional problems in relationships with our own kind, it's common to find emotional security, for a while at least, in the safer, less demanding, unconditional friendship of a dog. For many, disillusionment with human relationships, or reluctance to mix with humankind in general, can lead to the development of great bonds with animals, though, sadly, some people then restrict their emotional commitment solely to their pets and can become reclusive. The only way then for them to gain more emotional feedback is to acquire more and more pets. This can lead to the situation that we've probably all encountered where individuals own vast numbers of animals, well beyond the number that they can care for sensibly. They certainly have far too many for an individual relationship to exist with each of their 'pets', which in truth have become little more than a zoo-like collection of domestic animals.

Cuddly, fun and friendly our pets may be, but humans they obviously never can be . . . such are the thoughts that go instantly through my mind when I prepare myself for a carefully considered conversation with owners such as Mr Arthur. But I was in for a surprise . . .

'I'm a great believer in allowing Robbie to do as he wants and to grow up without controls and, as he's never been a nuisance to anyone, I must say I'm rather proud of him and the way he behaves. I'm pretty sure he's human really.'

So far so good. Mr Arthur, like so many confused people, actually sounded very erudite, considered and intelligent in justifying his approach to life with his dog and, as Robbie seemed to be perfectly well-behaved, who was I to suggest otherwise . . . except that Mr Arthur had only phoned me because of a problem with Robbie.

'You may think I'm a little strange, Mr Neville, but I also believe that Robbie should be allowed to develop and express himself sexually as a normal dog, especially at the present time because he is clearly an adolescent and will be responding to his hormones.'

'Well that's okay,' I said, 'providing he isn't causing you or your friends or their dogs any problems and . . . ' but I didn't get to finish.

'I've been allowing him to mount me to relieve his sexual tension, just on the arm in the evenings and it seemed to help him relax,' blurted Mr Arthur, having summoned up the nerve to face down the main issue. 'Problem is that he used to only want to do it about twice a week. Now he's onto me two or three times per evening and has taken to mounting my shoulder and head rather than my arm. I've ended up with his penis in my ear. Now I don't want to upset him by pushing him off, and frankly I don't mind him doing this, though getting it in the ear is a bit much. I presume that he'll be less demanding once he's grown up but I'm worried that he's becoming obsessed by it and concerned that he now leaps on me from his favourite resting position on the back of my chair when I have guests. How do I make him more discreet and turn him down a little? Don't tell me to castrate him because I'll put the phone down if that's all you've got to offer!'

It was the psychiatrist guest in that famous episode of *Fawlty Towers* who looked at Basil Fawlty, rolling around maniacally on the floor in front of him, and then turned to his wife and said, 'There's enough for a whole conference in that one.' There was certainly enough in Roger Arthur's attitudes and Robbie's behaviour to fill this book, and, though I was initially a little suspicious about the call, it certainly wasn't a hoax, as I found when I went to see the case at Mr Arthur's very plush, elegant Sussex home. There was Robbie, driven by innate and powerful sexual urges common to many adolescent male dogs, and then there was the outwardly respectable and accomplished Mr Arthur, who was so desperate to be the most accommodating owner possible and so dependent emotionally upon his dog that he allowed him to mount him. I'm not sure who was the more confused of the two, and it took a lengthy painstaking consultation with Mr Arthur, explaining the behaviour and sexual drives of dogs, before I could persuade him to take any sort of action at all. Even then, to go with the minimum of readjustment to their relations that Mr Arthur would tolerate, Robbie only received a very necessary anti-male hormone injection because the effects would be temporary and because I managed to convince him that his dog was in a terrible state of confusion through being given the right to mount his pack leader. I came away from the house absolutely exhausted and thanking my lucky stars that I could concentrate on Robbie's behaviour and not, as a human psychologist would have to do, wrestle directly with the intricacies of Mr Arthur's mind. But if this case sounds like the roughest end of the job, at least Mr Arthur was a passive participant in his dog's sex life. Believe it or not, a couple of years later, a much worse case of a pair of confused owners of a hyper-sexed dog was to appear at one of my clinics, as we shall see in Chapter 5.

Of course, in considering the sexual nature of our pets it would be easy for me to stick to what is known scientifically. But that is not what my job is all about. It would be as unhelpful as simply castrating every male dog to cure behaviour such as aggression, leg-cocking or sexual excesses. What I am faced with in treating sexual problems with pets is the thin end of the wedge in our relationship with what are supposed to be domesticated animals, an often unforeseen and invariably unwanted aspect of a pet's behaviour within an otherwise usually platonic friendship between man and beast. My job is to provide a reasonable explanation of what the dog or cat or rabbit is doing and what drives it, physiologically or

socially, to behave in such a way, and tailor a treatment plan that takes account of the owners' feelings towards their pet, their expectations of their relationship, their lifestyle and the family's opportunity to carry out my suggestions.

Robbie was, until his owner intervened personally, typical of some male dogs in some human packs who, lacking the opportunity to meet many of his own kind, attempted sex with his owners. Usually this occurs, as with my dining companion, with a woman or girl in the house, but more often the dog is aware that it is not his prerogative to attempt such things with his higher-ranking owners, male or female. So, if the cat won't stand still for long enough, the dog is very likely to pursue a catchable, inanimate object. The range of fancies in this area is enormous, as we shall see later, but favourite targets are soft toys. Nice, attractive, malleable, non-protesting, seductive, grippable toys.

The Bloodhound and the pink elephant

Such was the case with Gerald, a wonderful young lollopy Bloodhound who had fallen totally head-over-heels for a large fluffy pink elephant. He would lie by it all day long if given the chance, and then, every once in a while, mount it with a tender passion that is not normally the preserve of randy male dogs. The problem was that the cuddly pink elephant was also the favourite toy of Amanda Lacey, a sweet little five-year-old girl, who demanded to know just what Gerald was doing riding on the back of her toy with that fixed and purposeful expression all over the folds of skin that jingled around his face independently with every thrust he made. Amanda's parents sent me a simple letter having run out of comments like, 'Gerald thinks Trunkie (the victim elephant) is another doggie, darling. He's just playing,' and watching Amanda grow ever more suspicious that there was more to this than mummy and daddy were letting on.

> *Dear Mr Neville*
>
> *Our dog keeps bonking our daughter's pink elephant. Please help . . .*
>
> *Yours sincerely*
>
> *Maria and Karl Lacey*

This was a sad one, apart from the incredible sight of such an amazingly designed dog doing such rude things to something as bizarre as a large pink elephant. There was a perfectly reasonable explanation. Gerald simply never met any other dogs. He was a totally humanised pet who, on the face of it, lacked for nothing from his human pack mates. They had a large house for him to pad around in and a huge garden to romp and play in. There was even lots of wildlife trailing scents through the garden at night for Gerald to put his redoubtable nose to come the morning and track their paths as if engaged on the criminal detection work that his breed is famous for. He was lavished with the best food and attention, was kept in the peak of health and had plenty of opportunity to play and socialise with his owners and their friends. But he had never left the property since the day he arrived about three years earlier. Though the Laceys knew full well that dogs are pack animals, they had presumed that they were Gerald's pack and could provide all the social contact that he needed and that, because he looked so healthy and seemed so happy, all was well.

For the most part, owners like the Laceys will get away with that approach, pity though it is. But every so often, the basic drives of the pet dog may surface, particularly when it comes to sex for the male dog in the human pack. Gerald's drives were telling him to find a mate and, as most successful breeding male wild or feral dogs or wolves will do, establish a close pair bond with a suitable bitch within the pack. The couple spend lots of time together at rest and play and, in a stable pack, are usually faithful to one another for as long as the relationship lasts, which can be until one dies or the male is usurped from his position in the pack and his place taken by a younger fitter male. But, while the relationship flourishes, the male will mount his partner whenever she comes into breeding condition and that's how puppies are made. The problem for Gerald was that, aside from having had no opportunity to learn how to socialise with other dogs or develop courting skills, there was a limit to the intensity of the bond he could forge with any member of his human pack. Internally, this fit healthy male was being cued to seek a mate and establish a close pair bond as the best prospect for reproduction. Externally, his pack mates had rejected any such advances during Gerald's adolescence and remained firmly in control, as most owners are, of the scale and type of their dog's social interactions with his pack. Gerald had long ago realised that there was no prospect for forming a breeding bond with his human pack mates and he never met any other dogs in the local park to attempt even the early stages of courtship, let alone find access to a willing bitch. So, that most fundamental of the drives which direct our lives, the urge to reproduce, had nowhere to go for Gerald and was redirected onto the best alternative available, Trunkie.

Helping suffering owners come to grips with having their 'best friend' castrated is simply part of my job on occasion, as however much I try to avoid the surgical

option, sometimes it does prove necessary for peace to prevail. It may also be a kind operation to suggest for dogs like Gerald who live happy lives as pets but with entirely human packs where the owners' socio-sexual behaviour dictates and necessarily restricts their opportunity to express their own. For Gerald, castration would simply help relieve the frustration of having little or no opportunity to indulge in any form of canine sexual posturing, or sex itself, with his own kind. Just a few weeks after surgery, Gerald's fixation with Trunkie had evaporated and he was a far happier and less forlorn dog.

I always feel sorry for dogs kept under such circumstances, despite the excellent care that is lavished upon them. The price for them of being a pampered pet for mankind is castration, and though they may not suffer from the emotional consequences of it in the same way as a man would, if owners such as the Laceys could have a better understanding of the social needs of their dog, perhaps it wouldn't be necessary in so many cases.

If only owners like Gerald's could realise that most of his basic social drives are still wild and unchanged from his ancestors', despite the fact that a Bloodhound is about as far as you can get from the wolf blueprint. If only they could accommodate the fact that the dog is a sociable animal and needs to meet and socialise with other dogs because not everything he is designed and evolved to expect can be provided by human pack mates. Then they may just see a dog whose social excesses, including some of the sexual ones, would be better regulated and who would probably be even more fun to own. Had Gerald met lots of other dogs regularly, he may, like most males in a pack situation, have come to recognise that he was not one of the few high-ranking dogs who can establish the right to make a pair bond with a bitch and go on to breed. If so, his hormonal and emotional status may have adjusted and switched off much of his sexual drive, which may just have carried through to his home life and made him less frustrated. Mother Nature is, after all, the decider of who should breed and is far better and far more subtle at it than man.

As it was, the vet decided Gerald's reproductive fate and he was changed from being a dog with a strange fixation for a pink elephant to an asexual, but still very playful and trouble-free pet . . . which is no more and no less than what his owners had always wanted. The biologist in me would like to have seen him remain 'entire', given a little help with some behaviour modification techniques and offered lots more opportunity to be a dog, and be appreciated for it, before the surgeon's scalpel appeared. If it had worked, the Laceys may just have had the best of all worlds: a dog that didn't fancy their daughter's toy elephant but who remained fully male in the total repertoire of his behaviour. But then, wanting only a pet, not a wolf in their living room, they probably wouldn't have appreciated it anyway.

Sterilisation is also the price of a comfortable life in man's den for most cats of either sex, a few buck rabbits, and most bitches. But, for the vast majority of pets, sterilised or not, their sexual fate and associated behaviour is already decided on the day we take home that warm bundle of fluff to live with us as part of a human family.

And, except for those deliberately selected by us to perpetuate more of the same of their breed or type, that means a totally sexless lifestyle. But as we dart between the excesses of humour, sympathy, sadness, frustration, outrage, misunderstanding and incredulity caused by our pets' sexual expressions within the lifestyle that we impose on them and our ability to cope with it, there are, I hope, a few things to ponder on. The case of Gerald the Bloodhound reveals, I hope, the need for a greater understanding of the demands we place on our pets and just how much we expect them to modify their behaviour to fit into our homes. We'll also look at bizarre true-life cases of what we might all too easily call sexual 'deviance'.

As well as offering 'biological' explanations of my clients' pets' behaviour and sympathetic understanding, the pathway to the successful treatment of the sexpest pet and restoration of a happy relationship between the animal and its owner often lies through humour. Regaling clients with tales of owners like the Lacey or Thomas families who have suffered with other and worse sexual excesses in their pets helps to lighten the load with their own, and I have no hesitation in including the 'best' of my encounters with the sexual side of pets in this book, even though you'll require a fairly warped sense of humour to laugh at some of the sadder cases.

Of course, any excursion into the potentially dangerous area of animals and sex is destined to run a difficult pathway and, as I try to steer a respectable course, I'm well aware that this may be the last book I ever get to write. But then sex, after all, is simply the behaviour that all we mammals must go through to reproduce our species. Biologically, it's a miracle. Socially, it's a tightrope. Behaviourally it's hilarious and a constant reminder that the good Lord has a sense of humour! So let's take a quick look at the miracle and get it out of the way so that we can walk the tightrope and get on with a bit more of the fun!

1
Driven to Sex

'To live is like to love — all reason is against it, and all healthy instinct for it' SAMUEL BUTLER

All animal species, including our own, are born with unshakeable instinctive drives. The will to live and reproduce is fundamental. Why we are all here in the first place is a matter for wonderment and our various religious beliefs usually encompass our attempts to explain our own existence, both in terms of origin and raison d'être. But it is only because we upright apes have evolved such a hugely advanced brain compared with even our nearest relatives in the animal kingdom that we are able to consider such complex questions of philosophy. For sure, our cats and dogs do not spend long hours discussing the conflicts between religious fundamentalism and Darwin's theory of the origin of species nor worry about their relationship with their creator. For them, and all other life-forms, life is a 'here and now' event and their behaviour is simply how they respond to surrounding goings-on as best they can in an effort to ensure that they survive to reproduce themselves. Indeed, dangerously leaving aside the question of whether there is a God, one might, as many learned biologists have done, suggest that our bodies are simply life support systems for our genes. That in reality all plants and creatures are simply here to ensure that their nucleic acids perpetuate themselves; that in effect we are simply self-replicating chemicals allowed a brief moment of self-awareness to carry our genetic pattern forward in time.

It's a bit of soulless theory but when all is said and done, we are alive for but a brief blip on the universal timescale and our thoughts, philosophy, technical achievements and ability to manage our health and living conditions have yet to break us free from the inevitability of our death. Our individuality dies with us, but our genetic material survives in our children and our whole lives are unquestionably still shaped by the need to ensure its survival. Compared to the processes of evolution, our own desires as individuals are barely relevant.

The key problem facing any species is how each individual, each gene vehicle, can live long enough under the prevailing environmental conditions and within the limits prescribed by the design of our bodies, shaped by the experiences of preceding generations, to reproduce. The survival drives are already coded within our genes, perhaps constituting the true original computer programme from the gods. While some simple life-forms reproduce themselves identically through simply dividing in two or fragmenting, higher forms of life require two sets of independent genetic material to come together. A central activity for such life-forms thus involves locating a mate to gain access to compatible genetic material, but other behaviour such as courtship to encourage mating becomes a major preoccupation for all creatures, second perhaps only to the process of feeding, to ensure that we can fuel the drive to mate and reproduce . . . and all within a short time-span before the grim reaper arrives.

The behaviour of the higher mammals in terms of

survival and reproduction and their various systems of communication is especially interesting, and while our own is more complex than any other animal on the earth, that of other social mammals is also extraordinarily intricate. Indeed, it is extremely difficult to relate much of what we and the higher mammals do on a day-to-day or hour-by-hour basis back to the fundamental need to survive and reproduce our genes on anything other than the broadest of scales. Many of the things that we humans do in pursuit of business or pleasure, for example, seem to put our very survival at risk, yet we pursue actively the thrills of mountaineering or bungee-jumping or flying around the planet in aeroplanes. We humans, in the west at least, have been able to control our lifestyles, adjust our living conditions to suit us with our heated or air-conditioned dens, travel despite bad weather, ensure year-round food supplies and maintain physical health for longer than ever before compared to our ape ancestors or even our own of a hundred years ago. Protected somewhat from the immediate continuous pressure of having to adjust our every action simply in order to survive, we now have lots of free time to indulge in activities that make us feel good and develop our intellect simply for the pleasure it brings. And those who feel best perhaps live longer and mate more, despite the apparent dangers we sometimes subject ourselves to.

Our discoveries about our genetic background are, of course, very recent indeed. We've only known about DNA for forty years or so and, though we seem to be getting closer and closer to understanding the structure of life, we still understand very little about how genes work and are as far as ever from answering the fundamental questions of why life evolved and what it is for in the universe. Our pets, especially those such as cats and dogs which are highly socially interactive with us, now also live longer than ever before, benefiting from the improved health care, nutrition, and social and environmental protection that we have developed for them. It's just that they don't know it! But then our advances in terms of technology, longevity or social infra-structure are of no consequence to our pets whatsoever. We take them in and they exploit the situation, reacting happily to take best advantage of what we foist upon them. For them there has been no concomitant rise in self-awareness or appreciation of abstract pleasures to go with their new-found lifestyles. They are, as they have always been, simply here to survive to the best of their abilities and reproduce themselves, according to the master plan.

Out in the jungle, the forerunners of our pets had no problem with fulfilling the basic demands and purposes of being alive. The original ancestor of all our pet dogs is the wolf, while our modern-day cats are still pretty well genetically identical to the African Wild Cat that first moved in with the ancient Egyptians, despite over three thousand years of living alongside man in various cultures and climates around the world. Wherever the modified wolf or the African Wild Cat has found himself and however man has tried to shape them both into new forms to suit the demands of domestication, the basic drives of both beasts have remained absolutely unalterable. Fast asleep on a nice warm pet bed hanging off the radiator the cat may be, snoring in front of the artificial coal fire the dog may be, each safe from threats and stuffed full of the best prepared pet food that money can buy, but their genes are absolutely unaffected by our generosity. And their behaviour, though it has been modified particularly in the case of dogs to fulfil man's demands of his companions such as hunter, guard or stock herder, still largely obeys the basic need to live long enough to reproduce, no matter how comfortable the bed they find themselves lying on and however far from potential mates they may be forced to live.

But just what controls these natural drives and instincts that all animals are born with and which seem to govern the basic premises of existence, irrespective of lifestyle? Ultimately our behaviour and that of our cats, dogs, rabbits and all other creatures is controlled by the brain and the nervous system, the communication and information feedback system with the rest of the body. That control relies on inbuilt, inherited biological rhythms and the processing of the body's reactions to external goings-on in the environment. Information about environmental changes is gathered by the body's sense organs, ears, eyes, nose and skin, and transmitted as electrical pulses along nerves into the brain which decides what to do with it all and co-ordinates the body's responses. Depending on what type of environment and social system the animal has evolved to live in, some of the senses will be more sensitive than others and the power of the central co-ordinating brain obviously varies from a few neurons grouped together in simple animals such as flatworms to the billions that comprise the mammalian brain. Some of the mammals can even do without one of the senses altogether, for instance those that live in dark caves or underground have no need of eyes. But for sure all creatures that require two sets of independent genetic information to come together in order to reproduce must have a suitably advanced sensory system to be able to locate a mate in their environment. Some creatures rely on the sense of sight for most of their information gathering and mate-finding, while others, such as our cats and dogs, also rely heavily on their highly evolved sense of smell, a sense that is not well developed in their owners by comparison. But whether mates are located through sight, sound, touch or smell, the brain's prewired instinctive drives will usually organise the appropriate mating responses once one is found.

Another slower means of transmitting information

and controlling organs throughout the mammalian body and one which has more prolonged effects than those produced by the nervous system is the production of chemical messengers called hormones. The endocrine glands, situated throughout the body, produce and release hormones into the bloodstream. These are remarkable chemicals, because minute quantities can have dramatic effects on the function and physiology of the target organ or tissue in another part of the body. At any one time in our bodies, and in those of our cats, dogs and rabbits, millions of chemical and electrical messages are travelling around and their complex interactions and effects are what ultimately decides how we all behave.

Most bodily functions that are vital to maintaining our bodies while we go about the business of reproducing ourselves, such as breathing and heartbeat, have a basic rhythm that is varied automatically in response to external changes or internal demands. For example, all mammals automatically release the hormone adrenalin from the adrenal gland into the bloodstream in response to environmental threat or danger detected by our senses. Adrenalin increases our heartbeat and breathing rates and prepares us for action by supplying the body with more oxygen and pumping it to our muscles so that we can produce the extra energy needed to fight the threat or run away from the danger: the 'fight or flight' reflex. Breathing and heart rate also increase when we are active in direct response to the increased oxygen demand of our muscles and tissues.

Hormones, once released into the bloodstream, could potentially have any effect on any organ in the body. However, they only produce effects in certain target organs because only they have special sites on their cell walls, called receptors, that can combine with the hormone. Each receptor has a unique shape and can interlock only with substances of a specific shape —just like a key in a lock. As soon as the key is in position, chemical reactions begin to take place within the cell itself; for example, the production of other hormones such as oestrogen. Oestrogen can induce cell division and thus growth in other tissues by combining in turn with other receptors in these cells. Every cell has a great number of different receptors on its surface and it is one of the great biological wonders that each substance manages to find its way through the soup of organic compounds that surround each cell and get to the right place. This is all under the control of a special gland called the pineal gland found in the middle of the brain. The ultimate purpose of all this control is to achieve something so miraculous as the ultimate production of young versions of the adult.

In the wild, the survival of newborns is dependent on the availability of a ready food supply. Animals born in times of plenty stand a far better chance of survival than those born when food is scarce. The greater the extremes of temperature or climate, the more important it is for any animal to time its breeding season accurately. The survival of many species, such as the Arctic Fox, in cold climates is dependent on their ability to time reproduction according to the seasons. Such timing is also under the control of a particular endocrine gland found in the middle of the brain, called the pineal gland. This gland is proportionately larger in animals such as foxes and seals living in cold climates compared with animals living in equatorial climates, such as elephants. It monitors the length of the day and night, through a strong nervous link with light-sensitive cells at the back of the eye. The intrinsic rhythm of the chemical messengers released by the gland varies with the periods of light and dark in a day and, by monitoring the changes in hours of daylight, the gland acts as an internal body clock, marking time and the changing seasons. It also receives information from other areas of the brain that monitor temperature by collating information from temperature sensors in the skin.

The pineal gland co-ordinates nervous and hormonal control of the reproductive cycle and switches it on and off according to the seasons. When most active it secretes the largest quantities of a substance called melatonin. This inhibits the reproductive cycle, but when day length and temperature indicate that it is the appropriate time for the animal to breed, the pineal gland is least active and secretes lower levels of melatonin. This enables the reproductive cycle to commence and the animal to enter breeding condition. As environmental conditions may vary year by year, the system can adjust to ensure that the production of young coincides with best available conditions, including favourable climate and availability of food. For example, the Great Tits in Wytham Woods, near Oxford in the United Kingdom, usually lay their eggs in April following mating correlated with hormonal changes induced in the birds by the increase in average daily temperature and day length in the preceding month. If spring comes early and the average temperature reaches a critical threshold earlier in March, the eggs are laid early in April, but if spring is late, laying may be delayed by up to four weeks, into early May.

Cows, humans and most rodents can reproduce at any time of year but most other mammals have definite breeding seasons during which the female is physiologically able to conceive. The timing of the breeding seasons is variable according to the species. Most have one breeding season in the spring or summer while others, including most dogs, have two breeding seasons or, occasionally, three. As with some birds, the development of the reproductive system can be artificially stimulated by increasing their day length. Others, such as certain species of worm, are affected mainly by the cycle of the moon. The Pacific Palolo Worm spawns exactly one week after the November full moon, but if that appears bizarre, it's worth remembering that the sexual cycle of women is based on a lunar month of twenty-eight days.

The fact that in most breeds of dog, our pet bitches now come into breeding condition twice per year is a significant alteration from the reproductive cycle of their ancestor, the wolf, and with other wild canids such as the African Hunting Dog. The wolf bitch has only one cycle per year, though the timing of this varies between the twenty-three sub-species according to local conditions. It's a trait that probably evolved because the environment, lifestyle and heavy parental investment in raising the young dictate that only one litter is likely to survive. Interestingly, some 'older' dog breeds such as the Basenjii also only have one cycle per year, perhaps because they are still more closely related to the wolf, having been less altered since they were domesticated than others. The sexual cycle of some dog breeds may be caught mid-way on the road to developing two cycles per year as they presently only cycle every nine months, but in the original wolf, the production of young is so geared that they enter the world when the climate and food availability are optimal for their survival, an opportunity that only occurs once during the annual cycle of the seasons. Whether cubs are born to huge black Timber Wolves in Canada weighing up to 100 kilograms, or their brownish grey Spanish cousins weighing as little as 20 kilograms, the physiology of reproduction is the same and whether our pet dogs are, as some believe, derived from several wolf sub-species around the northern hemisphere, or solely from the smallish Asiatic Wolf of the near east, it is man who has altered their sexual cycle. As with most species he has domesticated, he has sought, through controlled breeding, to increase their reproductive output. This is achieved through shortening the time between birth and sexual maturity, increasing the number of sexual cycles to be able to produce more offspring per year, and increasing fecundity, the number of offspring produced per birth. It's interesting to note for a moment that probably the only reason that man can achieve these changes in the wolf-dog is because his aims are identical to those of the animal's genes, to reproduce more.

Our cats, on the other hand, have not been so genetically manipulated in the course of their relationship with man. One only has to compare the variation in the appearance of the dog, Chihuahua to Great Dane or Old English Sheep Dog to Dalmatian, all of which we have created from the wolf, with the greater similarity of the cat breeds to see how much more resistant to the normal consequences of domestication the cat has proved. After all, Siamese and even Persian cats are very similar in size and body shape to a moggy or crossbred cat. In fact, as I argued in my last book, *Claws and Purrs*, our pet cats are probably still almost genetically identical to what we have always presumed to be their ancestor, the African Wild Cat. The exceptions are the genes that code for coat colour and hair length which are, in any case, naturally highly variable in most wild cat species and easily manipulated by us. Yet reproductively speaking, while most of the twenty-six small wild cat species found around the world have only one, or, very rarely, two sexual cycles per year, each of a ten-day duration, the pet cat commonly has three, even when feral. In fact many pet cats can be more accurately regarded as polyoestrous, having continuous cycles of heat until they become pregnant. The sexual cycle is triggered at the beginning of the year by increasing day length in late winter and early spring but when the female pet cat is kept permanently indoors in the warm and under artificial lighting, the sexual cycle can continue throughout the year, even into the winter. The female of the wild rabbit, a species famed for its fecundity, also continues to have oestrous cycles throughout the year, once started, until pregnancy is achieved and can even conceive again about twelve hours after giving birth. The process of nursing one litter while pregnant with the next continues until the day length shortens at the end of July in the United Kingdom, and the temperature decreases. The pineal gland switches back on again in earnest to ensure that reproduction cannot occur in the winter.

We'll look in greater depth in the next chapter at exactly what happens to our pets' behaviour when the female cat or dog comes on heat, both in terms of their attempts to secure a mate, and also in terms of the mate-seeking, courting and mating behaviour of the other half of the reproductive scene, the male. But for now, it's worth bearing in mind the state of confusion that our cats' and dogs' ancestral hormone systems, biological clocks, rhythms and altered sexual cycles must be in and the biochemical strain that their physiology must be under when they share our homes as our pets. It's no wonder that their sexual behaviour can sometimes be rather strange and that's even without considering the often very strange expectations and social customs of their owners.

2
Pet Facts of Life

'Anyhow in a corner, some untidy spot, where dogs go with their doggy life' W H AUDEN

There are probably over two million species of animals and plants living on our planet today, of which the mammals are the most successful of the larger animals in our current era. Huge reptiles have had their day and long before any form of animal life evolved plants had the planet to themselves for eons. While man is undoubtedly the most successful creature that has ever managed to shape his surroundings to his own advantage and forge his own lifestyle, if not his ultimate destiny, many other mammals have also enjoyed an extremely successful time, at least until man started to over-exploit things. The obligate predatory cat and predatory/scavenging dog family are enormously successful animals and perhaps it is no mistake that even after hundreds of years of persecution of the wolf, the related African Hunting Dog and other canids, and our decimation of tigers, leopards, lions and their smaller relatives, we choose examples from these families as our modern companions.

We also keep plenty of cage animals, pets such as rabbits that we usually don't have quite the same intensity of social relationship with, but which nonetheless allow us to enjoy physical contact and which can, if we handle the domesticated version from an early age, at least regard us as non-threatening food providers. The rabbit is a good example of another extremely successful opportunist mammal. The ravages the wild version has inflicted on what were rabbit-free countries such as Australia after being introduced by man bear testament to the success of the basic design. Through swift adaptation to local conditions and, by 'breeding like rabbits' as only they know best, this sweet-looking creature has been able to colonise virtually anywhere that has suitable grazing. While man has readily domesticated the rabbit for food and altered its colour, size and shape to keep it as a pet, its performance in this role differs from cats and dogs. Though there is a growing trend towards keeping rabbits as indoor pets (they can be trained to use a litter box if you start early), they are generally kept outdoors as they simply do not adjust their general behaviour sufficiently to bring their keepers any increased reward from having them in the carpeted den. Though social in order to provide strength in numbers in the wild, the individual rabbit has not needed to evolve many investigatory skills to locate its food or relate to its own kind compared with the predatory cat or co-ordinated hunter dog and so is less interactive with its keepers.

Numbers of pet dogs and cats, if not rabbits, now far exceed the residual populations of their ancestor wild forms. If a large population is the main criterion of success of a species, then clearly the association of both cats and dogs with man has been a good move from their point of view. I once gave a lecture about the origins and domestication of our pets to a philosophical society in the north of England and I thought I'd start with a question that would lead me into a discussion of the origin of species and how man first waters wild animals down genetically in the course of domestication. 'Have you ever considered why we are all here?' I asked, trying to sound intellectual among some very intellectual company. 'Because we're not all there!' came the gruff reply from a man half-way back, a man clearly cajoled into attending by his pet-mad wife. He may well have been right from the human point of view as we could all have been standing at the bar at the time and enjoying ourselves. But from our pets' ancestors' point of view, his unkind interruption (which, incidentally, caused a huge laugh) held some truth. The price of domestication for the wolf is that as a dog he is now only genetically 80–85 per cent of his former self and though some of his capabilities have been enhanced by us in certain breeds, such as speed in the Greyhound, strength in the Rottweiler, strength of bite in the Bull Terrier, none of our wolves are as balanced and as generally competent as a hunter/scavenger as the model forged by Mother Nature.

The cat has fared better in his relations with man, managing to exploit the opportunities perhaps to greater effect and without much loss or manipulation of his wild genetic integrity. But both species, whether fashioned into strange and diverse shapes and sizes like Bulldogs, Irish Wolfhounds, Chihuahuas or Poodles, or our Persian or Siamese cats, the horribly deformed Munchkin or the quilted coat Rex breeds of cat, still bring to us the majority of their innate ancestral drives intact. The fulfilment of those drives behaviourally-speaking may be more than difficult since we started playing with the flesh, that is the genes that code for their physical appearance, but the spirit is as willing as ever to obey the command of the genes — go forth and procreate — and we seem unable to alter that.

Rabbit rabbit

While we have been able to produce about forty very attractive pedigree strains of rabbit and quite a variable size difference between the dwarf varieties and the huge Flemish Giant, most rabbits are still kept in an outdoor hutch and run and so perhaps are less likely to have confused physiologies than our cats and dogs indoors. Additionally, rabbits are usually not neutered as a standard procedure and so remain far more true to their wild ancestors in terms of sexual development and behaviour. Of course, all rabbits need to experience being handled and gentled from an early age to remain friendly as adults but aside from the odd scratchy one that missed out on early gentling, I've yet to see a doe with any behavioural problems at all.

BUNNY BOYS

Dear Mr Neville

Recently my daughter's white rabbit, Dylan, has become something of a tyrant. I realise that he's probably matured into a full male this spring, but he's become very difficult for her to handle. He used to be happy for her to pick him up and put up well with being lugged around (not by the ears, I hasten to add). Now he struggles fiercely and, once on the ground, becomes extremely active and rather aggressive if pursued. Is there any reason for this sudden transformation and is there anything we can do to bring back the cute little bunny in Dylan that my daughter used to enjoy?

Yours sincerely

Alexandra Kelsey

Bucks quite often become problematic as adults, despite plenty of early handling. The difficulties usually start in the spring, as with Dylan, and there's a very good reason for it. In as much as wild female rabbits are fertile through a breeding season from late January to about the end of July in the United Kingdom, males also come into breeding condition at about the same time. Between August and January neither sex is in breeding condition and so litters born towards the end of the season are unlikely to reach sexual maturity themselves prior to the following January. For pet rabbits, this can mean a long period of being very gentle and easy to handle in the same way as peace prevails in the wild rabbit warren at these times. So it can come as quite a shock to owners of pet bunnies like Dylan to find them suddenly becoming full-blooded males as their testes descend and start pumping out the testosterone in response to the same cues of temperature and day length as trigger their wild cousins. If the rabbit is also a dominant character (as a result of, or caused in part by, a high male hormone output) then the behavioural consequences of being in breeding condition can be all the more severe. In a wild colony, a rabbit like Dylan is quite likely to be a high-ranking buck in what is usually a linear hierarchy of male importance. High-ranking males tend to be heavier, tougher and maintain rights of access to better feeding areas, shelter and, most importantly, to the does. His job would be territory defence and he would be generally rather intolerant of other members of the colony approaching him. Strangers would be driven off with quite fierce displays or attacked physically, bitten and kicked if they didn't withdraw. It may well be that Alexandra's daughter is being seen as an occasional member of the colony by Dylan who objects to the effrontery of having his status challenged through her advances. What may have been acceptable social interaction a week earlier may suddenly have become a challenge, hence his reluctance to be picked up and tendency to become aggressive if pursued.

The testes of many male rabbits are withdrawn back into the abdomen during the winter when they are very much out of breeding condition. The increased temperature in the abdomen keeps the animal sterile and lowers hormone production, which in turn can cause a decrease in the buck's boldness and secondary sexual characteristics. In short they can become nice pets again, but only until the next descent of the testes. In cases where males are seasonally nasty, I usually recommend that they be castrated by the vet, though of course this has to carried out when there is something to remove for simplicity of surgery and reduced risk, compared with going into the abdominal cavity in search of testes which are much smaller than when they are in the scrota on the outside. If it sounds odd to be castrating an animal that is more widely regarded as a pest or farmed for food than kept as a pet, it's only a sign of the times. We want our pet rabbits to be friendly, and just to sit out their lives largely untouched, being fed and watered in a hutch. With such males the only other options would be an injection of an anti-male hormone, repeated every few weeks through the breeding season, or to keep him with a group of does and either sterilise them or find plenty of homes for plenty of offspring. Otherwise, the dominant and seasonally highly-charged buck like Dylan is a steaming train with no stations to stop at, and though it may be anthropomorphic to say so, it would be a lot less frustrating for him to be castrated and be saved all the bother. And naturally it should mean that he would be more likely to stay cute and handlable for Alexandra's daughter all year round, though there still may be seasonal changes in his behaviour under the control of other less well understood hormonal triggers and, as an adult, he may still be quite a tough character.

BUCKING THE ISSUE

Dear Mr Neville

Our male rabbit, Mac, really is quite a disgusting beast. Whenever we go into his run, he thumps his back feet on the ground in excitement, tries to chase us and has even mounted my childrens' legs when they sit down to play with him. While we keep his nails trimmed, this has caused some pain to the children and we now don't let them in with him unless we are there to supervise matters. Perhaps we will get them a female next time, but while this is a problem we can manage, what is most objectionable is that our dear little bunny insists on squirting the whole family with urine or something when we go into his run. He kicks his body round and just sends a great jet of the stuff in any direction, but invariably it lands on us. Should we just eat this rabbit and get another one or is there something we can do?

Yours sincerely

Mr and Mrs Clutton-Smith and family

This is another down side of keeping a highly charged male rabbit on his own, especially during the breeding season. Again the behaviour is normal and to be found in abundance in every rabbit warren at that time. When a buck rabbit finds a doe that smells and behaves receptively, he chases her for quite some time. Poor Mac, kept alone, simply views his owners as welcome company and chases them in an excited way. Thumping or stamping of the back feet on the ground is more often used at other times as a warning sound between rabbits, especially by wild rabbits living in large social groups and for whom early recognition of any threat is crucial if they are to run underground to avoid it. Pet and wild rabbits also stamp when excited, especially sexually. By circling or pacing in front of his owners as well, Mac is going through the rituals of courtship, another feature of which is the display of the white underside of his tail. Usually does play hard to get for a while, but eventually allow themselves to be approached. If there is a delay or the buck is particularly excited, it is all the more likely that he will send a jet of urine at her as he runs past, a behaviour which she tolerates in the build-up to mating but which doesn't exactly cause her to give him a huge immediate 'come-on' by lying down with her ears pressed back flat, or by flagging her tail in reply. Only when she's ready will she give the signal for him to approach and nuzzle her prior to mating. But, after all this activity and urine squirting, the act of mating is surprisingly quick, and the male invariably ejaculates after just a few rapid thrusts. Interestingly, it appears that bucks actually lose consciousness for a few seconds as they ejaculate.

From the Clutton-Smiths' point of view, it's not much fun being the damp targets of Mac's peculiarly rabbity foreplay and more painful actually to be mounted, so it's probably wiser again for Mac to take a trip to the vet and have his breeding seasons shortened to nil with the same operation as should befall Dylan. It's either that or he's for the pot . . . which reminds me of the friendly and sexually quiescent rabbit owned by a friend of my wife. He was called 'Dinner', which is probably what kept him on his best behaviour and his anatomy intact.

Pussyfooting

The female sexual cycle, or period of oestrus, could be generally defined as that period of time when the female allows the male to mount and mate with her, and it is only during this time that she can become pregnant. The oestrus cycle itself is controlled by the level of a number of circulating hormones, some derived from the pituitary gland in the brain, such as follicle-stimulating hormone which facilitates the development and release of an egg in the ovaries. The ovaries themselves produce two hormones, oestrogen and progesterone, the relative levels of which control the sexual cycle. Oestrogen is the main sex hormone and is produced at a relatively high rate until just prior to ovulation, the release of the egg from the ovary into the fallopian tube ready for fertilisation. At this point the level of oestrogen falls sharply but prior to this it has already caused the uterus to become prepared for the fertilisation and implantation of the egg. If this all reads like the usually well-thumbed reproduction section of a school biology text book, then it is simply to elucidate the miracle of co-ordination of the sexual cycle of the female. As well as causing such marked physiological changes, the high level of oestrogen also has some very pronounced effects on the behaviour of the female because it is vital to find a male to fertilise the egg or eggs at exactly the right time. The limiting factor of sexual reproduction in nearly every species is the receptivity of the female while males, as we'll see later, are usually ever-ready, given the right stimulus, and will fight for access to, or should it be 'the privilege of mating', a receptive female.

Just prior to ovulation the relative level of oestrogen falls as the level of progesterone rises, this hormone helping to ensure that the cells of the uterus thicken and provide sufficient nutrition for the egg, and to promote the development of the placenta once a fertilised egg has become successfully implanted in the uterus after mating. Both hormones also play a role in preparing the mammary glands to produce milk so that in the event of a successful pregnancy, the early food of newborn mammals will be on tap. If mating is successful in any mammal, a third group of hormones are produced by the placenta. This is the structure which connects the foetuses to the womb and enables them to derive nutrition from the mother's bloodstream and which later also takes over the production of progesterone from the switched-off ovaries to maintain the continuing development of the uterus and prevent further menstruation. Smaller amounts of oestrogen are also secreted, though the relative production of the two hormones reverses again as the time to give birth approaches, often also with necessary accompanying behaviour changes.

Clearly both female hormones have broad-ranging effects and influences on the whole reproductive process from mate attraction to birth and, interestingly, the human contraceptive pill uses the effects of artificially manufactured progesterone to achieve its effects. By raising the level of progesterone artificially, development of the cells that surround each egg being shed in the ovary is suppressed and the body can be fooled into thinking that it is in the early stages of pregnancy. Thus the sexual cycle is suppressed to concentrate on ensuring the successful growth of the egg implanted in the uterus . . . except that there isn't one there. Of course, such chemical contraception is also possible for our dogs and cats to enable us to manipulate and control their breeding, an influence we shall explore further in Chapter 6.

CATCALLS

Dear Mr Neville

We have a beautiful eight-month-old Siamese female cat called Chloe. On the advice of her breeder who says she is a perfect specimen, we intend to breed from her when she is old enough, perhaps in a year or so's time. We were expecting to have her first season about now but were advised not to have her mated until she is much bigger and more mature. We were warned to expect her behaviour to change a little at this time from the cuddly kitten we took on a few months ago and to expect some noise as she calls for a mate . . . but really! Chloe has become a total tart — soliciting outrageously by rolling on her back and sliding her tail and rear end past our noses if she gets the chance to jump up onto our laps or if we are sat at the table. She knows no bounds in her desperation and virtually begs everyone and everything, including our poor deaf, blind, fifteen-year-old spayed bitch Poodle, to mount her. We are, of course, keeping her indoors at this time so that she doesn't meet up with a wandering tom and get pregnant, and while we can live with her outrageous flirting for as long as it takes to pass, we are going crazy with the calling. She's so loud and so frequent, on and off through all hours of the day or night. Is it normal to be so vocal? Is there anything we can do to switch Chloe off apart from putting her in a sound-proof room? Help!

Yours sincerely

Angela Williams

The word oestrus comes from the Greek word *oistros* which means 'mad desire' and most female mammals show heightened sexual excitement in their behaviour during this period as it is now that they must attract the attentions of a male in order to mate.

There are marked behaviour changes in the female on heat as Chloe has demonstrated all too well. The changes that accompany the period of sexual receptiveness in the female cat can come as a special shock to those owners who aren't expecting their pet to become an absolute whore, and even to those like Angela Williams who are well aware of what is likely to happen, but unprepared for the scale of it all. Queens normally have several ten-day cycles of receptiveness per year and clearly demonstrate that they are sexually available by three main means. Physically they roll on their backs in an extremely provocative fashion, which is instantly recognisable in humans but interesting from the cat's point of view because they mate with the male mounting the standing or upwards lying female, not in the missionary position. During this period, the queen's vulva may redden and swell, though not to the degree observed in bitches. While she's on her back and wriggling, the queen may also paw frantically at the air or 'tread' her paws and call out with a wail that sounds like she is in mortal pain. Many inexperienced owners rush their cat off to the vet at this point only to be told the bordello truth of it all.

If no tom arrives as a result of all this signalling, the cat may go wandering aimlessly around the house, or dash outdoors if possible, still calling at the top of her voice in the hope that a passing tom may hear. In fact, assuming one hasn't been provided for the purpose, toms from far and wide are still likely to be attracted by the scent of the female on heat. Special sexual chemicals called pheromones are released from vaginal discharges and in the urine and faeces and, through their odour, are designed to induce sexual responses in the male. Indeed, many queens will now spray urine on scent posts at home and, if they get the chance, outside, to attract toms.

Pheromones can be detected in the air in concentrations of only a few parts per million by a tom, who may thus be able to locate the female by walking up the concentration gradient of the scent, sometimes starting from many miles away downwind. If a tom does arrive on the scene, the queen may go into more elaborate and lascivious rolling, but reject his advances until exactly the right moment for impregnation. Then, and only when she is absolutely ready, she will usually lie on her front with her rear quarters raised to be mounted. After all that you might expect quite a performance, but mating is usually very short and sweet, though it may be repeated several times or the queen may allow any other males present to mate with her as well.

So, the female cat on heat attracts mates to her with scent and sound advertisements and assures their attention with seductive behavioural displays. It's normal but I have a special sympathy for Angela Williams, having suffered from the sleep-wrecking, sanity-destroying ravages of not one, but two queens that came on heat together when our Lilac Point Siamese pair, Miss Bean and Flirty Bottom, did their stuff. As sisters still living together as adolescents, it was no surprise that Bean's and Flirty Bottom's oestrous cycles coincided, and no surprise that the high wail of the Siamese should be so loud and resonating as they began calling. What was especially annoying was that they were almost exactly out of phase in their periods of actual calling. Just as peace seemed to prevail after several hours of wailing for a tom by Bean, the never more accurately named Flirty Bottom would strike up, thus ensuring a rapidly declining desire to keep fertile queens in the anticipation of breeding from them one day. Indeed, as their desire to attract a non-existent mate got ever more desperate, our desire to keep them at all fell at an equal rate. Cat fan as I am, three successive nights with no sleep makes experiences over the past year with our baby daughter, Sinead, pale into nothingness and almost had me building them their very own shed on the other side of the old limestone quarry that our garden backs onto. I reckoned that a distance of about a mile would ensure that we couldn't hear them, whereas a night's 'holiday' for Sinead at the mother-in-law's is the most we've ever been driven to by a teething baby.

So, for owners like me, a single experience of the pitch and range of a calling cat's voice, or rather two when they are searching for a mate, convinced me to have them sterilised as soon as the vet advised, a process which stops the sexual cycle by removing the ovaries.

The reproductive hopes of Miss Bean and Flirty Bottom were dashed or, rather, excised by our local vet before their duet could ever be repeated, but if Angela, despite all, still intends to breed from Chloe, it may indeed be wise to build a separate breeding enclosure out of earshot in the garden or, as she suggests, a sound-proof room. There Chloe can 'do her thing' according to the direction of her sexual cycle and not disrupt life in the family den while she awaits the day when she will finally meet the tom of her life.

OUCH! SEX HURTS IF YOU'RE A QUEEN

Rabbits and cats are of particular interest in the reproductive physiology of the female. Unlike bitches, ovulation in the doe and queen is delayed until mating actually occurs, thus ensuring that the eggs are released at exactly the right time for the sperm which has been deposited by the male into the vagina to swim up the uterus to fertilise them. It's a sure-fire method compared with the rather less reliable process of ovulating first and hoping that a male will have mated with you at the right time to ensure that both egg and sperm can come together.

With rabbits, intercourse itself seems to stimulate ovulation in the doe, but for the queen things are a little more painful. The penis of the male has tiny backwards-pointing barbs which cause sharp irritation to the female's vagina as he withdraws after ejaculation. Invariably and understandably, the female screams at this juncture and lashes out at the male with a paw full of claws. An experienced tom can thus be seen to dismount very quickly with his head held as far out of firing range as possible, and who can blame him?

But the pain of his going causes a chain of nervous and physiological reactions that cause the eggs to be released from the ovaries about twenty-four hours later and thus, as sperm remains viable in the uterus for four to five days, almost always ensures that mating successfully leads to fertilisation and conception. Interestingly it also means that if the queen mates with several toms at a sitting, as often happens in groups of feral cats, then

individuals in the litter of kittens that she goes on to produce may each have different fathers.

Doggy style

Bitches normally have two cycles per year, each comprising four stages. During the first stage, called pro-oestrus, which lasts between six and eleven days with an average of about nine days, the vulva and surrounding skin swells and usually has a watery discharge, though the bitch will be unreceptive to males at this time. The next phase is oestrus itself which again lasts about nine days. Now during which the bitch is likely to urinate much more frequently than usual in an effort to broadcast her ready state on the wind telegraph. Now there is less volume of discharge but it is stickier and smells a lot more attractive to male dogs, as this is the only period when the bitch is receptive to being mated. The lining of the uterus becomes engorged with blood ready for the implantation of the egg and begins to bleed, which can be messy for the owner, especially with long coated breeds such as the Old English Sheep Dog, but provides increased visual signals for any nearby males and scent signals for those further off. A bitch in oestrus may also become an escape artist, willingly leaving home to go in search of males with whom she may become very flirtatious. If kept firmly at home she may instead solicit her human family and other people, often men, with a rear-end waggle and presentation, tail held neatly to one side to indicate her desires and facilitate mounting for you! Ovulation occurs spontaneously early on in oestrus, and as dogs lack the neat timing of egg release in response to mating in cats and rabbits, conception is a less guaranteed affair but more likely to be successful if the bitch is mated between the tenth and thirteenth days of the onset of the heat, rather than towards the end. If she isn't mated, a period of dioestrus follows, lasting about ninety days, when she will refuse to allow herself to be mated, though she continues to produce progesterone as the main sexual hormone for reasons that we explore further with the case of Helga in Chapter 5. The anoestrus period follows dioestrus, lasting about one hundred days when the bitch's sexual cycle is inactive, the hormone cycles are quiescent and everything returns to normal in preparation for the start of the next cycle.

The process, as we have discussed, is governed by the activity of the sex hormones and, just prior to the end of the cycle and the onset of menstruation, there are marked changes in relative levels of oestrogen and progesterone.

Without delving into the exact complicated mechanisms of it all, progesterone can have a marked effect on the mood of the individual woman or bitch, making her more relaxed and less reactive. If the fall-off of this hormone towards the end of the cycle is sudden, or the individual is especially sensitive, a period of great emotionality can result, with depression, temper volatility and unpredictability being common signs. This is, of course, known as pre-menstrual tension, a thing which no man ever gets but from which a great many men, as well as women, suffer.

PMT

Dear Mr Neville

Our Toy Poodle bitch, Mimi, suffers from what I can only describe as PMT. Every time she comes on heat, she seems to come under a cloud of depression. She's unwilling to go for a walk, can be extremely snappy towards us and generally just wants to lie in her bed all day. Sometimes she leaps out of her basket to try and bite us when all we are doing is walking past and this is in total contrast to her usual friendly character. Is this normal and is there anything we can do to help her?

Yours sincerely

Mary and Brian Hall

As well as women, many bitches suffer from PMT, my own lovely Cassie the nine-stone Bullmastiff included. In fact she used to become so depressed, lethargic and troubled-looking that we had her spayed for this reason alone, having been quite prepared to keep her cycling and fertile in case we did want her to have a litter at some point. So if it isn't absolutely essential for the Halls to have a litter

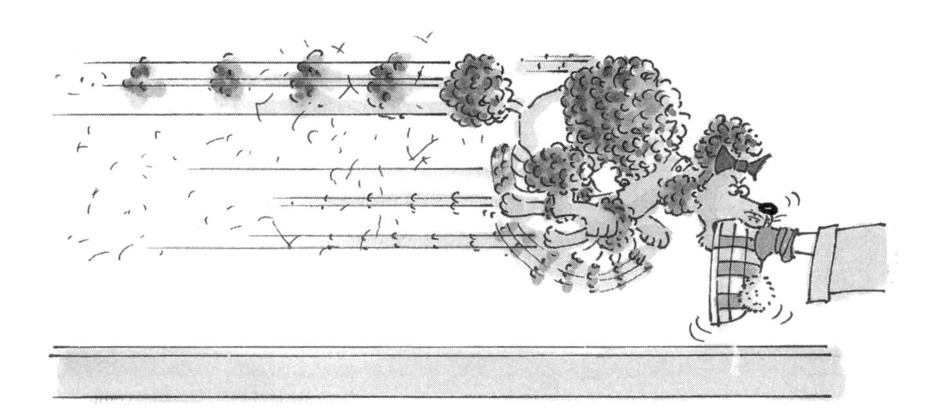

from Mimi, then they could save her a lot of distress and themselves a lot of worry and careful treading around the house over many years by asking their vet to spay her.

A man's world or a dog's life?

In the human male as in other mammals there is no sexual cycle, but the activity of the reproductive organs is regulated by hormones from the pituitary gland at the base of the brain in the same way as the hormones of the female respond to environmental, sensory and emotional cues. The mechanisms are very complicated but one hormone seems to promote the manufacture of sperm in the testes, while another causes specialised cells there to secrete androgens, the male hormones. Androgens are chemically rather different from the oestrogen and progesterone of the female and their main function is to stimulate development of secondary sexual characteristics which, in man, means body hair, a deep voice, muscling up of the body, etc. In many mammals they also make the male more competitive and territorial, and active in terms of mate searching and the desire to mate — given the appropriate cues — and thus testosterone has a direct influence on male behaviour and character development as well as on the physical appearance of man or beast. It is this more direct effect on behaviour as well as easy access to the site of production that has caused many males of many species of pet and domestic animals to be castrated as part of our general husbandry practice to make them less competitive or easier to handle, again a phenomenon of our relationship with our pets that we shall look at more closely in Chapter 6. Adult tom cats and male dogs are sexually active and ready to respond to a sexual opportunity until the day they die, though there may be some loss of libido or sexual drive as they age.

DOGGED BY A SEX PEST

Dear Mr Neville

I breed and race Whippets and, to be quite frank, they mean more to me than anything else in the world. I'm very proud indeed of my dogs' performances and especially so of 'Hare Raiser Flo Jo' or 'Jo', which is her pet name. She is not only a grand champion racer herself, but many of her puppies have turned into champions and nearly all of them have done very well as racers. I only breed once every two years from her and try and match her to the very best stud male Whippet available at the time to help ensure that her success continues on. My problem is trying to ensure that when she is in season but not going to be mated by a Whippet that she stays unmated by other dogs. I keep her in, walk her only late at night on a lead and have made my garden like Fort Knox. But, despite all, there is a male Labrador, a real old slobberer, who lives just down the road from me who comes calling every time he finds her scent on the wind. This dog's name is Pest, and never was a dog more appropriately named. I don't know how he does it, but he manages to get in my house and at my Jo every time she's on heat. He's come over the garden gate, so I built it higher; he's dug under the fence, so I dug it two feet deeper into the ground and just last week, I stopped in the street with Jo on the lead to talk to my neighbour, turned round and there was Pest, come out of nowhere and already on her back. Believe me, I've tried to ask Pest's owner to keep his dog in and under control, but though I honestly believe he's tried his best, there seems to be no way to stop Pest once my Jo's on heat. How can I persuade him to have Pest castrated?

Yours sincerely

Malcolm Postlethwaite

Good old Pest! He was one of those lovable old rogue Yellow Labradors, and was actually owned by my landlords when I was at university in the north of England in the late 1970s. Their surname was Waters, and so their dog's pedigree name was Tempestuous Waters, or Pest for short. He was a big-chested strong-running dog who always had a glint in his eye and who loved nothing more than to chase the ladies of the canine kind around the neighbourhood. Most of the year it was just social calling and for the most part Pest confined himself to dallying but platonic encounters with bitches during walks around the village and in the fields and countryside nearby. But, without fail, for the two and a half years that I lived with the Waters family and their dog, every time Jo the Whippet came on heat he was away. All he needed was a chink of light in the door frame, an unguarded moment in the garden or the car window left open and out he slipped, as quiet as the night. Mr Postlethwaite's protestations about Pest's courting of his prize Whippet had begun several years before I arrived on the scene, as soon as Pest had come of age and found Whippets especially to his liking, but it was clear that all attempts to be reasonable had died in the frustration of trying to cope with a randy, insistent Labrador.

I can't remember just how many times an irate Mr Postlethwaite banged on the front door grasping Pest unceremoniously by the collar, his doggy penis still slightly protruding, but I do remember vividly the night when Pest had gone missing again for just a few minutes and, in a short time, had obviously achieved his aim in life and managed to mount Jo and 'do the job'. The thundering on the door of Malcolm Postlethwaite had brought us bleary-eyed to receive our good neighbour's account of Pest's latest exploits in his efforts to create a new breed of dog: a thinnish, greyish golden wedge-headed mutt with great big soft eyes, that runs like stink! 'Yon bloddy Labrador's bin at my prize Whippit agin . . . y'ought to cut 'is bloddy grahpes off!' He shoved Pest inside with the side of his boot, though with surprising restraint, given the circumstances, and we made our usual humble apologies and vowed to keep the village's yellow sex fiend in for a few days as best we could until temptation had passed.

Once Postlethwaite had gone, we sat down and simply laughed until we couldn't even imitate the first three words of 'Yon bloddy Labrador's bin . . .' any more and the tears ran uncontrollably and breathing became difficult. Pest, the placid family pet, who had not an ounce of nastiness in him, who never did anything undesirable at home of a sexual nature and who regularly curled up asleep with Polly the cat, had won again. Even though castrating him would perhaps have been kinder for Jo and made life when she was on heat less frustrating for Pest himself, and certainly easier on poor old Malcolm Postlethwaite, his sex drive, the changes it brought to his innocent disposition, and the repercussions of it all were just too good to miss. Pest and his seasonal pursuit of Jo were part of village life and, as only one person was really suffering, and far more people were deriving great enjoyment from his sexual forays, he remained a complete dog all his life.

Pest lived out his last years in mid-Wales to where my old landlords, Olive and Peter Waters, moved for some peace and quiet after their own kids, their foster children and students had finally all moved out. Detached from his favourite Whippet by about a hundred and fifty miles, Pest had to make do with local 'talent' until the end of his days. True to form, and despite rickety legs and difficulty in walking, he was seen hard at it with some flighty but very willing collie-type bitch in the town square at the ripe old age of thirteen on the day before he died. Perhaps that was what finally finished him, a case of 'a bitch too far' but it seemed a thoroughly appropriate way for the old trooper to go. Mr Postlethwaite, a man who would never forget what it was like to suffer from the attentions of a male dog calling after his bitch, probably held a party.

Pest was proof that though the flesh may be weaker in the older dog, the spirit is more than willing, and the body, given the opportunity of a willing partner who isn't too far off the ground for your back legs to cope with in your old age, will always do its best to respond to those innate drives to pass on your genes as often as possible. And 'one last go and out' doesn't seem too bad a way to go when the flesh finally can't cope with it all!

Of course the male of the species, be he cat or dog, can show far more excessive sexual behaviour than dear old Pest, and we'll look closer in the next chapter at the aberrant male when he is usually to be found at his disgusting worst, during his transition from puppyhood to adulthood in the crucial period of adolescence.

Anyone for sex?

The mating behaviour of cats and rabbits seems rather perfunctory. All that is required is a receptive female and almost any male will do. There seems to be little in terms of mate selection, though there is evidence from studies of farm cats that certain types of male are more successful at mating and therefore at fathering kittens than others. However, this success does not seem to relate to their dominance in the colony as apparently high-ranking toms will often be beaten to it, be displaced when mounting or simply be content to take a turn among many mating an oestrus queen. Early experience in mammals, especially the social ones such as ourselves, can have a profound effect on subsequent sexual behaviour as adults. Tactile contact with members of the same species during the non-reproductive period of infancy has been shown scientifically to be of great importance in rats, guinea pigs, cats and dogs. The awful and widely publicised experiments with infant monkeys isolated from their mothers and denied the opportunity to touch her or any other of their kind, showed all too unpleasantly just how any social animal can suffer if not given sufficient tactile and social contact when young. Failure to mate as an adult is just one of a range of physical or psychological disorders that can result from a deprived upbringing and exhibits clearly just how important relationships are in the reproduction of social mammals, including those adapted to be our pets.

NOT TODAY THANK YOU!

Dear Mr Neville

Many of our friends who breed dogs have stud males that perform anywhere with any bitch and are forever mounting things. But not our Belgian Shepherd Dog, Tristram, Mighty Baron of Avondale the Ninth, usually called Zak. Though he has won more prizes in the show ring than any of our other nine dogs and is in great demand, he simply won't perform at all at stud. He's been presented with a variety of attractive bitches of his breed, all at the peak time of their cycles, but he shows no interest whatsoever and just goes away and lies down. How can we turn him on?

Yours sincerely

Sarah and Jimmy Stewart

Mating is generally also commonly observed by us to be a rather straight-forward process as far as dogs are involved, but that is usually because we bring a dog and a bitch together who have been specially chosen for the purpose. In fact, in a wolf, wild dog or feral dog pack, there are complex social influences at play to decide which dogs mate and thus in whose puppies the whole pack will invest energy and commitment in raising. Free-living packs are highly social, living in often clearly defined hierarchies governed by very highly developed behaviour. While for much of the time in their day-to-day behaviour, the hierarchy is not important, it is nonetheless established to enable the group to decide which dog has access to what and in what order to prevent potentially injurious conflict between them, especially when competing over a limited resource.

Hence the dominant male in a pack does not maintain his position by periodically beating up all his underlings, but is boss because the others acknowledge him as such and allow him access to anything he chooses to demand. He is clearly more likely to demand access to food when it is in limited supply, or access to the best shelter when he is too hot or too cold and his rights to these resources are predetermined so he can take them without a fight. The hierarchy is regulated by many complex factors of which we understand but a few and misinterpret far more, but an individual's age, sex, physical condition, hormonal status, relationship with certain other key individuals in the group and sexual state will all affect his or her position. This position varies according to circumstances far more than we often realise.

In wild dog and wolf packs it is often the case that only the top-ranking bitch and male breed, a situation achieved partly by the male establishing a close pair bond with his mate and spending most of his time in close proximity to her, and thus denying others access simply by being there and making them unwilling to challenge him in order to get to her. Naturally, the alpha male, as he is often called, becomes more insistent about maintaining his rights of access to the alpha bitch as she comes into season and though others may be tempted to approach more when she is receptive, if he is successful at keeping them at bay he will ensure that she ultimately selects him to mate with and thus produces his puppies.

Other members of the pack hunt to feed the puppies and provide necessary protection, not just because there is strength in the larger, strong pack that will result from their successful upbringing, but because most members of canine packs are closely related already and a high percentage of any member's genes will be the same as the alpha breeding pair and their offspring. Thus, to protect the puppies is to protect the survival of each dog or wolf's gene line even though there is no direct involvement in the puppies' conception for the majority of individuals in the pack. It's a case of survival of the strongest genes being the key factor, and in the dog's social set up this means a reduction of importance of most individuals in terms of the demands to be reproductive. Our pet dogs are, of course, less rigidly influenced by such group considerations and few dogs enjoy such a socially closely regulated sex life. Few pet dogs ever form true breeding pair bonds within a pack. Very few indeed will mate for life, and most of those used deliberately in breeding will get to mate with a variety of partners while forming enduring social relations with hardly any of them. The canine drive to reproduce is clearly strong enough to overcome the social etiquette of mating found in the ancestral wolf pack, otherwise we wouldn't have so many dogs as pets!

Indeed, given the willingness and ability of our pet dogs to reproduce so successfully and to levels well beyond our control in most countries, it's interesting to note that most wolves in a pack will effectively be non-sexual and may ignore any sexual cues that surround them. Unlike our free-spirit, humanised dogs, they recognise from their established position in their pack that they have no right to mate. If they tried they would be seen to be challenging the alpha dog for his position and may risk serious repercussions. If this resulted in injury, this in turn would weaken the pack as a hunting and puppy protection unit, which would not be in that low-ranking individual's best interests. Hence he avoids all these problems by not putting himself forward. Zak is probably one such dog. Because he is kept effectively in a small pack containing higher-ranking males and accepts his low-ranking position in the hierarchy, he wouldn't dream of putting himself at risk by attempting to mount a bitch. That is the preserve and privilege of the dogs higher placed than him. It all sounds undemocratic and in human terms it probably is, but whoever said that dogs should be democratic in the first place? They have a perfectly evolved social system that served them extremely successfully for thousands of years and meant that dogs like Zak could live successful and untroubled lives while contributing to the success of their pack and helping to carry many of their genes forward to future generations. We all too easily feel sorry for the lower orders in a pack, for the ones who don't compete, who cringe deferentially when a high-ranking pack member approaches and who don't want to mate, but we shouldn't. No dog suffers by being of low rank, in fact their acceptance of it keeps them out of harm's way on the

inside and protected against threat from the outside.

Zak's relations with his pack are right for him, and it's just tough on his owners that he won't perform. Their appreciation of his qualities in terms of physical appearance and performance in the show ring have no bearing on him or his behaviour whatsoever, he's sticking true to his canine programming. Of course, if the Stewarts want him to breed, they should certainly make sure that no other males are present when they want him to perform and perhaps even keep him as the only male, and thus dominant in his pack. Removing him from the other dogs altogether and thoroughly humanising him may also help his canine instincts to become less influential when he is subsequently introduced to a suitable bitch. But care is needed here too as dogs who view themselves very much as part of a human pack can often have problems when they are suddenly expected to behave as dogs, especially when it comes to mating. After a life of communicating as best they can in human terms, such dogs often lack the social skills to relate to their own kind and functional impotence, usually due to anxiety, is just one of many sad consequences. But even for a dog that is socially very competent with other dogs, familiarity with the bitches in a group can occasionally diminish the male's sexual interest when one comes into season, even if he is apparently the dominant or only male in the 'pack'. This gives us an indication of just how affected by social influences the whole process of mating must be. In such cases the potential mates are best isolated from each other for a week or so, so that the reintroduction is more highly charged, like the sailor arriving back home after a long voyage. Introductions for Zak to a potential and willing mate should also be carried out on neutral ground or at the bitch's home to preclude any reluctance to perform that has become directly associated by Zak with his home and social position there.

Success for Zak's owners in getting him to mate may

also depend on the lucky bitch's perception of her right to solicit a mate if she too is of low social standing in her own pack and her coming into season is being seen as an affront to more dominant bitches when a strange male arrives on the scene. Some bitches may even perceive themselves as so socially low-ranking that at the sight of a full blooded male approaching them, even when they are sexually receptive, they submit totally by rolling on their backs . . . and dogs can't do it like that! As with her counterpart male, but due more to the effects of her physiology than her social behaviour, the alpha female is often the only one to be fully active in the pack in her sexual cycle and thus the only bitch available to the alpha male, which also ensures the survival of her genetic investment in their offspring. It seems that there is some cunning mechanism evolved in stable packs whereby the pheromones released by the breeding bitch during her cycle cause a physiological suppression of the cycle of most or all other bitches in the pack, though the exact means of this are unknown. Some bitches still cycle but not so strongly and are far less fertile, though this may be indicative of a less stable pack or a relatively newly formed one which hasn't had enough time to establish all these inter-effects to their fullest extent. That the cycle of one female of a social mammal species can affect another is clear, however, and nicely demonstrated by the synchronisation of menstrual cycles that was observed in women employed in typing pools in the 1950s and 60s. On top of all this 'science' there's the fact that some stud male dogs will only mate with certain individual bitches and reject all others, and some bitches will only allow mating by one or two males. Dogs, after all, are entitled to the luxury of personal preferences more than ever if they are forced to live and breed under a deregulated sexual code as human pets rather than under the tight socio-sexual control of the canine pack.

The cubs or puppies produced by the alpha pair in a

wolf pack are likely to be stronger than puppies produced by any other mating within the pack and are more likely ultimately to go on to breed themselves. Thus the fittest survive, as demanded by Mother Nature, but the realities of the law of the survival of the fittest are far more complex than in the basic simple underlying theory. Of course, no social system can be rigid and everlasting for any group. The old must move over for the fitter young to come to the fore and maintain the pack's strength. Previously sexually inactive individuals, especially sub-adults, may still be strongly motivated to rise in the pack's hierarchy and, upon attaining top position, come into breeding condition immediately. Similarly, injury or prolonged absence of the alpha figures may cause temporary social instability and allow previously lower-ranking individuals to come to the fore. It's all very fluid and very complex when we attempt to relate all these influences into the situation of the modified wolf in the human pack. There are many, many variations and confusions on the original theme that can occur, especially when there are only one or two canine members in the pack, as we shall see in Chapter 4.

Tie me up doggy style!

For those unused to the sight of dogs having sex, it never ceases to amaze just how they get into that final position, locked in the 'dog-tie' standing rump to rump in what must be the most impossible position possible! Though the male mounts the female from the rear, once inserted in the bitch's vagina, his erect penis becomes still further enlarged by the swelling of two glands at its base, called the bulbs of the penis — which are not to be mistaken for testes. This swelling locks him in place, at which point he casually steps over her back with one of his hind legs and puts it on the ground, exchanging places with the other foot and his penis remaining all the while firmly inside her. The two lovers stand rump to rump for about half an hour, before his erection finally subsides and they separate, he none the worse for his strange position, which, we are assured, evolved to maximise the flow of semen into the bitch. The 'tie' is not essential for fertilisation and pregnancies can just as often result from the preliminary mounting. This is known in the dog breeding business as 'slip-servicing' and is about the most justified and supportive case for premature ejaculation that I have ever heard. For a creature with a forward facing penis, the 'tie' position is nothing short of remarkable and, as a human male, I cannot tell you how delighted I am that sex doesn't involve such elasticity of one's pecker!

But barbed tom cat penises and dog-ties apart, it's now already clear that many stresses are placed on our dogs, cats, rabbits and other pets in the way they try to adjust to life in human company and especially in our dens. On the one hand we want them to behave in a socially acceptable manner when we've had the decency to bring them out of the jungle into civilised surroundings, and we would very much like them to put away beastly things in favour of a more genteel lifestyle. After all, we'd

probably like to think that there's no need for them to hunt if we feed them, no need to go socialising or having arguments of a territorial nature when we apparently give them all the food, shelter and social contact they require of a home base. And we'd certainly like them to forget about the need to look for a mate or do anything of a sexual nature because they are there in our homes as our companions and there is surely no need for them to worry themselves about reproduction unless we decide that we need some more of them. But on the other hand, it's not so easy for our cats and dogs simply to brush aside the fundamentals of life and the indelible hormonal, nervous and physiological adaptations and biological rhythms that govern how they behave. While we have deliberately bred our pets to favour some of the genes that code for their appearance or tweaked some to make them slightly less reactive and more docile with us or less competitive with their own kind, the genes and rhythms are still in there, instructing each little furry vehicle to stay fit and reproduce itself. Sometimes the basic system appears, causing havoc with our social rules and civilised expectations, even though we invest so much effort in physically managing their opportunity to reproduce or curtailing it altogether. For sure, our pets can't help it, but for most of us it's only when the aggressive side of our cuddly pets appears or, perhaps worse, when the ordinarily dormant sexual side rears its shocking ugly head, that we realise the mistake we have made in assuming that a pig in a mansion can behave in any other way than as a pig, albeit a more placid, friendlier and arguably prettier pig than his ancestors.

3
The Pains of Adolescence

'... he stood trembling with pubertal confusion on the brink of life' STEPHEN FRY

The influence of the pineal gland, the gland in the brain which controls reproduction, is not only seasonal, but also triggers the onset of that most amazing of periods in any mammal's life, puberty. From birth the pineal gland has been very active in the young animal and suppresses the release of hormones from the pituitary gland that would stimulate the development or growth of the sexual organs and associated secondary sexual characteristics, such as muscling up of the body in the male and development of the mammary glands in the female. But the pineal gland monitors the passing of time and, at the age coded by the animal's genes, it becomes less active, the 'capping' of the activity of the pituitary gland is lifted and some of its hormones stimulate the onset of puberty. The resultant hormonal changes that mark the onset of sexual maturity and the cyclical changes in the female reproductive cycle are governed by internal biological rhythms which are influenced or triggered by external factors such as temperature, season of the year and social opportunity if, like the wolf or Chimpanzee, the animal lives in a group.

The age at which an animal reaches puberty varies according to longevity of the species, the way in which a particular breed or sub-species has evolved to live in a certain climate and, in cats and dogs, it is relative to the size of the breed. Both of these species on average enter puberty at about six to ten months of age, while we longer-lived humans reach it at the age of about twelve years in girls and fourteen in boys when eggs or sperm can be produced for the first time.

The exact timing of the onset of the remarkable changes that occur at puberty varies between individuals of course, but one of the most noticeable effects of puberty is a sudden spurt of growth. For the male of any mammalian species, puberty also brings a surge in the production of the male hormone, testosterone, from the rapidly developing testes. This initiates the sexual drive and excitability of the adolescent, be he a boy coming into manhood, a male puppy becoming an adult dog or a male kitten turning into a tom cat. The brain of every male is masculinised just before birth with a surge of testosterone produced by the mother. Hence little boys, male dogs and male cats are often quite distinctly male in their behaviour, for example in their relative competitiveness over trophies or toys, even well prior to the onset of sexual maturity and the production of testosterone for themselves. Male puppies are not only more competitive in their play than their bitch counterparts, but because of the effects of the testosterone received from their mother, also mount all of their litter mates far more frequently.

By contrast pre-pubescent girls and female kittens and puppies are not so overtly female in their behaviour as they receive no pre-natal surge of female hormones from their mother and oestrogen and progesterone will only affect their behaviour and sexual cycles when they begin to produce them for themselves at puberty. Pubescent females also grow quickly at this time and are approaching their ultimate full adult height and weight at the time they enter their first sexual cycle. Bitches of the larger breeds of dog tend to enter their first season much later than the smaller models and often as late as eighteen to twenty-four months of age.

The sexual drives of people, cats, dogs, in fact all mammals, become apparent in the adolescent period and it's a confusing time, as any teenager can tell you. Caught between kittenhood and being an adult cat, or puppyhood and being a grown up dog, it's not always an easy time for either our pets or we owners as we all struggle to cope with changing relations. For male pets especially, the rush of testosterone produces new and overwhelming feelings of sexual excitement and the desire to experiment with them, to learn the tricks of the trade of becoming an adult. Sometimes the adolescent male just can't help the responses of his body, but whereas his social gaffes as an immature child or puppy or kitten were forgiven by adults or companions, once he's an adolescent, he starts to carry the can for his actions and must learn to control his developing physical sexuality. Growing male dogs and toms simply respond to what their changing body tells them to do, and the production of the highly influential hormone testosterone can vary by the hour at this time. It undergoes some enormous surges and can cause some enormous responses.

BEN THE FLASHER

Dear Mr Neville

Our one-year-old male Dobermann, Ben, is a regular source of embarrassment. Almost every time he sits down with the family in the evening, he displays what nature has given him. He shows no shame as he sits there 'in extensum', in fact, if anything, he looks a bit confused by it all and wears a look of blank surprise, though with a slight glint in his eye, I'm sure. We usually try to distract him with a game or a fuss or, if we have company, we turf him outside to cool off for a few minutes. Is his flashing likely to develop into more assertive sexual behaviour, such as attempting to mount us or lead to aggression of any sort and, if so, should we be thinking in terms of having Ben castrated now to prevent these things from developing? Or is he just growing up and can we expect that he will grow out of being a flasher given a little time?

Yours sincerely

Martin and Annabelle Shore

There's little better designed to shock in polite company than a dog's erect penis. Call it what you will, his lipstick, pencil or pork sword, it's a bludgeoning contrast with its normal asexual appearance, packed neatly out of the way in a little furry or inoffensive skin sheath, and almost out of view under the walking or resting prostrate dog's body. It's as polite as you get for its most-used function of peeing out of, indeed, the dog even lifts his leg to get it in the right position to urinate from. But when he is sitting up, lying on his side or on his back with his appendage in an engorged state, a dog's penis is about the worst thing in the world. And it's always there, pointing, when there's a lady in the room or when the kids are playing. My nephew can't be the only five-year-old in the world who, convinced that it's far more important than the adults are making out and unwilling to be brushed off with 'oh that's only Ben's tummy banana' has had the facts of life explained at an earlier age than his parents had planned!

Immediately the thing hoves into view, we're into a potential minefield of social problems and not just with the kids. Depending upon the adult company we're in, our male dog's erection can cause laughter, embarrassment, awkward silences, a pronounced effort not to look in the dog's direction and acute self-awareness about what those people to whom we've only just been introduced must think about us. While the sensibilities of a lady unused to dogs might be rather mortified by our big brown Pointer's great red pointer and cause her to turn a similar shade, others of the fairer sex more used to animals may simply laugh its appearance away. But there can be few men who, even if outwardly trying to hide their embarrassment, don't wonder for a moment just why the canine male got to the front of the line when the big willies were being handed out. The male flea that may lurk in the dog's coat, however, puts his host proportionately to shame with one of the largest sexual organs relative to body length in the wild world. The flea 'penis' is twice as long as its body, but size probably still doesn't count, even for a female flea, when it comes to reproduction.

Relatively, male dogs, and especially the little breeds, do seem to have done very well indeed in the genitals department, but the real professional 'dirty raincoat' breeds tend to be short-haired and large, such as Dobermanns, Dalmations and Weimaraners. If ever we needed a reminder of what dogs are here for, the flasher illustrates very graphically that the male of the species can be very reasonably described as a life support system for a penis!

Martin and Annabelle's questions regarding Ben are not too easy to answer for certain at his age. It's unlikely that his behaviour will lead to him becoming aggressive as a more adult male, though, equally, it is often true that male dogs which are aggressive towards their owners in challenging them for position in the hierarchy of their pack, are also often quite highly charged sexually. But

then that's what you'd expect from a high-ranking male as one of the privileges of rank is that he would expect to breed and will look for mates. But the majority of male dogs are not motivated to seek high position in the human pack and are rarely aggressive towards their owners. As adults they are also very unlikely to make sexual advances towards them but they must still go through their adolescence when their hormone levels and desire to experiment sexually are vital for them to learn how to behave as adults and develop an appreciation of their rights and social relations. It may be that for a short while, Ben's learning processes could well include a few attempts to take sexual liberties with his owners, but he'll probably grow out of it all after a few months. Far too many owners have their young male dogs castrated at the first sign of unwanted sexual behaviour, and far too many vets advise the use of the scalpel before a dog has had the chance to adjust his new-found sexual motivations and responses within the context of his social group. Even if Ben proves to be an almost constant flasher, or develops more interactive sexual habits that become absolutely intolerable for his owners, I would still always advise a 'wait and see' policy for as long as possible. But then like most vets I'm opposed to recommending any unnecessary surgery as there is always some risk, albeit minor, with any general anaesthetic. In any case there are often other options to the knife, even with problems that start to involve the owners more directly . . .

SWEET DREAMS

Dear Mr Neville

Our young male Dalmatian, Piper, is going through that awkward age when his skin seems too big for him. He's now nearly fully grown physically but still behaves very much as a puppy for a lot of the time. He seems very confused by developments 'downstairs', especially when his 'old man' makes an appearance. He licks himself frequently but looks up at us in the process, apparently concerned about our reactions. We generally ignore him because it doesn't happen that often, and having watched our three children go through the pains of adolescence, we understand the confusions that go with this period of his development. Piper isn't a sexy dog and, so far, has made no advances towards us or anything else. However, last night he was lying asleep on the couch and seemed to be having a dream. His feet were twitching quite violently, his uppermost legs started to pace and his back seemed to be arching rhythmically. Naturally I was concerned that he may be having some sort of fit and so approached him to investigate and perhaps stir him a little before he shook himself off the couch. As I got near I saw that his 'old man' was 'ready for action', as it were, but as I gently nudged his shoulder, he awoke just in time to ejaculate all over my front. I don't know who was more surprised, Piper or me, but I can certainly tell you who was the butt of most hilarity from his wife afterwards! I've never heard of this happening in a dog before. Will he grow out of it, and is there anything we can do to help him through what I hope is a passing phase?

Yours sincerely

Gordon Mellor

Ahem! This was indeed the first and only case I had ever encountered in eight years of practice where a dog had what amounted to a wet dream. Of course, we know that adolescent boys can have erections and wet dreams when their rapidly developing emotionality spills over into their subconscious while they are asleep and sexual responses can occur totally involuntarily. But for Piper, a dog, to have an experience to the point of ejaculation almost implies that there were conscious processes of rationalisation that went through his mind when he was awake, mental erotic images perhaps, that passed deeper into his mind and came to the fore again when he was asleep to cause such a marked sexual response. That Piper's body could respond to internal hormone surges was not beyond doubt, and perhaps many dogs have an erection during their sleep or as they begin to wake as a straightforward physiological reaction without any apparent stimulation in the same way as when they are awake. But Piper clearly had very vivid images of something passing through his mind when Gordon went to investigate, and only a little more stimulation was required, perhaps just the physical process of stirring as he awoke, to make him ejaculate. Thankfully for Gordon, this was a once-only event, though Piper was, like Ben, something of a flasher in his adolescence.

Despite his damp and sticky experience, Gordon was unwilling to have his dog castrated, but when Piper became an almost compulsive flasher whenever he sat down, we did opt for an anti-male hormone injection for him. This was duly administered by the vet and repeated a couple of times over the next few months. The injection largely neutralises the effects of testosterone for about three weeks and takes the edge off behaviour related specifically to the action of the hormone. I figured that Piper's low threshold of arousal was due to his high hormonal status and this was probably the cause of his reactions in his 'dream', not the passing through his subconscious mind of attractive bitches, flirting irresistibly. They may have been there, after all who can really tell, but it was his hormones that produced his body's reactions. With them muted for a while Piper was indeed much calmer sexually, and by the time he was three months older his hormone surges had died down, their general level had presumably settled down to normal and there was no need for any further treatment.

Gordon was delighted that, despite the ultimate of indiscretions, Piper had not needed to be castrated, though everyone in the Mellor household made sure for some time that they gave Piper a wide berth when he was asleep and approached from behind to wake him if ever he was twitching in the course of less erotic dreams. Piper is now a lovely large adult Dalmatian, spots and all, and with all parts intact, but I fear Gordon will never live down his experiences of his dog's adolescence, though, like the offending event, he takes it all full on the chest like a man and laughs.

Although much of the reproductive drive of either sex, and especially during adolescence, is instinctive and can lead to inadvertent unconscious responses such as Ben's and Piper's, animals must also learn how to temper and moderate their sexual abilities and behaviour to

acquire the social skills necessary to locate and secure a mate (or mates) and ultimately go on to reproduce themselves. The expression of sexual behaviour will ultimately be determined in the adult by the combination of innate drives, hormonally inspired behaviour, reflexes, active use of the brain and the application of lessons which can only be learned through experience. Adolescence is the time when the experience must be gained about how to behave sexually and it is the social consequences of this experimentation that can cause many a confusion for the young and fast-changing animal. Social animals such as dogs, and especially male dogs, must learn now how to incorporate sexual behaviour into their overall behavioural repertoire.

Sexual behaviour figures little in the behaviour of a bitch until the onset of her sexual cycle. As we have seen, most changes occur in response to the relative levels and effects of the two main sex hormones, oestrogen and progesterone, and in the long anoestrous periods the bitch is in neutral regarding the expression of sexual behaviour. Males, on the other hand, are ready to operate at all times, given the appropriate cues from the female and in response to internal pressures, both social and hormonal. But as pack animals, dogs only survive because of their ability to communicate their intentions to one another and devise co-ordinated responses. And this is as true for sexual interactions in terms of courtship and mating as it is for hunting, puppy raising and shelter finding.

In fact for dogs, developing a sex life is a lot more difficult than for cats, whose general activities have been increasingly solitary since weaning. To achieve adult breeding status in the pack, a dog must not only mature sexually in physical terms, he or she must also mature socially within the dog group and attain a high enough rank among other adult members to establish the right to breed. And though much of the social advance occurs hand in hand with sexual maturation and, from the male point of view, the communicatory effects via scent and behaviour of rising and high levels of sex hormone on other males, much of it must also be vied for.

The puppy and young dog plays with its litter mates and, later, also with other young dogs in the pack to practise and mimic the social, physical and communicative skills of the adults it sees around it. It also learns how to communicate and be deferential to adults, especially towards its mother when being weaned, and it also learns that some adults, the high-ranking ones, are to be treated with more respect than the low-ranking ones as it experiments with various types of greeting, play and other physically interactive behaviour. Keen to experiment, playful, driven on by hormones and increasingly competitive, the adolescent dog starts to test his social and sexual skills with all members of his pack.

As social animals, adult dogs can be extremely tolerant of being experimented on by teenagers in their pack, but they do start to apply different kinds of limits on a young dog's behaviour than those they used with the same animal before he started to grow up. The new language of 'no' rather than 'now come on, pup, stop annoying me please' is one of the first to be learnt by the adolescent male dog who tries to mount an older adult bitch. She'll only allow so much advance to be made against her for the adolescent to practise and learn how to court a bitch and give him a chance to try out the behaviour, approaches and routines that will prepare him for adulthood. But when he looks like he's pushing his luck too far, he'll often be told in very definite terms that sex is not on the menu in his relations with this bitch.

It's confusing all right. After all, not a week ago, the puppy male could leap all over her and even go through the rituals of mounting without much rebuke unless he became really over-excitable and she'd had enough and wanted a rest. Now, he does exactly the same thing and finds that he's quickly deaf in one ear from the roar or growl of her disapproval.

Dogs must learn to manage their responses to competitive challenges and sexual advances, especially young dogs entering adolescence from about eight or nine months up to about a year to fourteen months in most breeds and types. At this age, they equate to the human fourteen- or fifteen-year-old in terms of development. Clearly the widely accepted view that one human year is equivalent to seven dog or cat years is a rather misleading over-simplification. It can lead to something of an early surprise to any owner who believes it and expects their kitten or puppy to stay young and innocently playful with no thought of sex until it is two years of age.

KISS ME, HARDY!

Dear Mr Neville

Hardy is my one-year-old Hungarian Vizla and he has a very definite eye for the lady dogs of our neighbourhood. Ultimately he may be used at stud with bitches of his own breed but he, of course, is unaware of our desire for canine racial purity. He is a terrible roamer and will happily escape at a second's notice, just when our back is turned, in pursuit of any local bitches. He has wandered several miles from home on a few occasions and could go further, I'm sure, if he caught the whiff of a bitch on heat. Thankfully we don't have to worry too much, because after climbing every mountain and fording every stream, and even finding his dream, he's always found dancing around his girlfriend like an idiot, play bowing and barking a lot, but not actually attempting to mate. He does stand there like a twit mounting the air but, so far, seems to have little idea of which end to approach and what to do. I suspect that Hardy will eventually get it right if given enough opportunity so we are building a more secure fence and gate to the garden, but is he likely to grow out of wanting to go a-courting without being castrated so that he can still be used at stud with his own breed later?

Yours sincerely

Nigel Durrant

The main problem for adolescent dogs growing up in the human pack is that they do not have the opportunity to experiment with many, or even any, other dogs and so are invariably removed from the constant feedback of response from more adult pack members about their experimental behaviour. Nonetheless they will be compelled by their hormonal status and changing attitudes towards other members of their pack, both canine and human, to experiment and try their best to learn the ropes. For males, as we saw with Pest in the last chapter, that may mean going away from the territory in search of opportunity and experimenting with totally unfamiliar bitches. Such bitches in the park are naturally less likely to be tolerant of the cheeky and clumsy assaults of a strange young male than a bitch who has been around him like an aunty helping him grow up in the pack. Our young dog may immediately try to mount any bitch that he meets in his excitement and not wait to see whether she is even interested in being friendly. A severe warning usually tells him that he's made a major miscalculation, but only after being rebuffed several times will he learn to be more cautious in future. Unfortunately the lessons learned may only apply temporarily and he may be just as keen on their next encounter in the park, or he may only learn to be more respectful towards the one bitch and require similar altercations with lots of others before the general message about how to approach the opposite sex starts to become ingrained.

Of course, our young male dog would learn a lot quicker about how to communicate with the opposite sex if he were living in a dog pack and interacting with other dogs constantly, but this is rarely possible at any stage of his life as a pet, as we shall see in Chapter 4. But even occasional encounters in the park usually ensure that he will come to read the signs of bitch-speak and take time to play and court any bitch that takes his eye — which usually means all of them — rather than simply throwing himself at or on them all. Providing the dog gets plenty of relaxed opportunity, he can be as social as the truly pack dog. What fills my clinics and those of my colleagues are those dogs, male and female, which sadly have been deprived of the opportunity to meet their own kind at adolescence and earlier. They are often aggressive or nervous and incompetent as dogs, both in terms of indicating sexual intent and in their general ability to communicate, as a direct result of living in a closeted, human-orientated pack.

Despite the lack of social opportunity the instinctive drive to interact sexually remains in dogs, undiminished from the wolf, as testosterone fuels the urge to roam in search of it. This urge may occur to extraordinary levels in many male dogs such as Hardy simply to help them seek out the opportunity to acquire experience, and even without the irresistible cue of the scent of a bitch in season on the wind. Hardy, responding to his new-found internal instincts, is probably only a few such experiences away and perhaps only needs to encounter a bitch in season to learn how to fulfil nature's sexual demands of him. Hopefully, Nigel will be able both to contain him physically and also to supervise many introductions to other dogs generally in the local park to satisfy some of the desire to socialise with other canines until the time when he is presented with a suitable Hungarian Vizla bitch on heat to mate with. There are, after all, far too many unwanted puppies in the world already fathered by escaping male dogs for Hardy to be allowed to carry on running off, and anyway, a Hungarian Vizla mating with anything else is likely to produce a very odd-looking, highly strung, very active and difficult-to-home litter of puppies!

MAKING ENDS MEET

Dear Mr Neville

My dog Duke is a Weimaraner and is a prime specimen of his breed. Although still quite young at two years of age, he has walked away with many, many prizes in the show ring and is now in demand as a stud. Duke is certainly keen to perform and though he gets a bit over-excited and sometimes needs a little calming down before he's let near the bitch, he soon tries to get on with the job. The problem is that he seems to find the bitches front end a far better proposition than the rear end, and, as you can imagine, his success rate is not high when it comes to fertilisation. On three occasions now he's started and 'finished' at the wrong end! I've tried to intervene to push him round to the right end of the bitch, but he gets a little aggressive and I'm loath to push him any further. Do you have any ideas of how to help him get it right?

Yours sincerely

Peggy Brayman

This type of problem doesn't usually fall into my area, in fact, I'm left peacefully alone by most of the dog show and breeding fraternity to concentrate on people who keep cats and dogs purely as pets. But Duke is a clear example of a dog who is responding to all the right cues from a bitch in season presented to him, and does all the right things, but at the wrong end. This isn't a case of a dog with a preference for oral foreplay, this is a case of a dog who hasn't had sufficient opportunity to learn through experimentation with experienced bitches how to get it right. It's simply that Peggy hasn't realised that social behaviour and sexual responses are closely linked in a creature as social as the dog and though most do okay, there will always be a few like Duke who haven't matured enough socially with other dogs to match their sexual maturity and willingness to respond to the irresistible come-on of a bitch in season. Though his sexual reactions are triggered by pre-wired instincts tempered by male hormones, Duke probably still has a little growing up to do in a canine social sense and would benefit enormously from being put with older experienced bitches to mate who will help steer him round and mate properly. Peggy may be able to restrict Duke's access to the bitches' front end only by holding her head through a hole in a board so that he can only get to the back, and he may then learn to keep on getting it right thereafter, but it would be far easier for him to benefit from a bitch or two of experience, if he is to be expected to pass on his qualities to lots of litters. Incidentally, interference from Peggy when he's already mounting, even at the wrong end, is seen as an unwanted challenge, so it's not surprising that he growls at her if she tries to push him (wouldn't you?).

While dogs such as Hardy and Duke would eventually get it right if they were living in a dog pack and achieved the right to mate, in a world of few canine companions the outlook is rather different for them and most male dogs of like mind. What our dogs encounter is not a range of adult dogs with centuries of evolution behind their understanding, tolerance and ability to communicate to deal with this stage in the juniors. Instead they find perhaps one or two other very humanised dogs in the home who may not respond in truly canine fashion to contribute to the young dog's learning. The probing adolescent also encounters a group of human pack mates who play by other, if often similar, rules and who may interpret his or her actions very differently when it comes to sexual, or what looks like sexual, advances and displays.

JUST BITCHING

Dear Mr Neville

Our Boxer bitch, Sasha, is very obedient and friendly but will keep presenting her rear end towards us whenever we try to fuss her. She hasn't had her first season yet and our vet says to expect it any time so we wondered if her behaviour is a sign of her oncoming change? If so, will she stop presenting herself to everyone afterwards because it's really quite embarrassing!

Yours sincerely

Alan and Gwen Kirkpatrick

Bitches give very clear-cut canine statements to nearby potential mates that they are at the height of their season and on the point of ovulating. The difficulty for we owners of bitches is that our pets will often also 'present' to us as part of their normal social behaviour. It's a form of gentle subordinate behaviour which is telling us that we have the right to attempt to mount if we choose, though the bitch would be most surprised if we actually followed up the option. It's a bit like the bank manager offering you an extended overdraft facility to show that he trusts you but which you ignore because, now you've got his trust, you don't want to put yourself in a position of him being able to call the tune because you owe him too much to manage safely. Such behaviour is only really possible between friendly pack mates when the bitch is actually in season, when she would present her rear end with tail aside to a selected male. Alan and Gwen, aside from being flattered by Sasha's confidence in them, may be wise to have their dog examined by a vet who may be able to detect other signs that she is about to come on heat, but if she isn't, then they should best ignore Sasha's actions, and certainly not reward the behaviour by stroking or fussing her. Instead, they should get up calmly and without a word walk a couple of paces away and call their dog to them. As she gets close, they should ask her to sit and then offer the patting and kind words that Sasha is seeking. That way she will learn to communicate in the way that Alan and Gwen want her to and as her rear end will be on the floor, she won't be able to wave it at them.

Generally bitches coming to season will become very playful, adopting the play-bow with forequarters down and rubbing and pressing their bodies against potential male suitors. They may also play more physically, wrestling and rearing up to box males with their fore-paws as a preliminary courting behaviour to mating. Bitches may also urinate more, and as deliberate acts of scent marking with perhaps a leg raised from the squatting position in a manner similar to leg cocking by males, to spread the message that they are about to become receptive. It's a time for any bitch to broadcast generally that she is available and so she may be easily excitable and bark a lot too, and also may be inclined to attempt to mount other dogs or bitches nearby as a sort of misdirected overspill of her excitement. As we saw in the last chapter, some bitches become depressed in the build-up to ovulation, but some may also become aggressive towards their owners or other dogs, especially in that often all-too-confusing first heat of the adolescent bitch. But, as ovulation finally occurs, they too will usually become just as willing to mate as any other bitch who goes through a normal excitable or playful build-up.

BOTTOMS UP!

Dear Mr Neville

Whenever we stroke our young female cat, Anna, she spreads herself flat along the chair or ground, arches her back slightly and sticks her rump in the air. She puts her tail to one side and seems to be making herself available to us sexually. The more we stroke her back the more excited she seems to become. Is this really a sexual reaction and, if so, why is she doing this when she hasn't even had a season? Surely she doesn't see us as tom cats?

Yours sincerely

Pam and Ron Smith

Cats also retain the sexual drives of their wild counterparts, not surprising when they are so genetically similar if not identical to their ancestor, the African Wild Cat. Most pet cats do at least have the freedom to come and go from the human den as they please and have more chance to interact freely with others of their own kind in the neighbourhood. Cats, however, are not pack animals when it comes to social relations with their own kind or in their hunting policies. So, if they are sociable with other cats, it is simply for the joy that the friendship brings, rather than for the increased success in hunting or better survival chances achieved by dogs living in a group. Sex for cats is not based on pack order as it is with dogs, nor is it much confused with general social behaviour. It's a case of each tom and each queen for him or herself. Their sex lives would be as unrestricted as their social lives were it not for the fact that we usually have them all sterilised before they reach adolescence. The timing of our intervention is often based on tradition, at about five or six months of age and just before the cat enters puberty, but is occasionally prompted by the earlier appearance of sexual behaviour as in the case of Anna. This is rather similar to Sasha's presenting behaviour in the previous letter, as Anna is very much adopting a position known as 'lordosis', the receptive mating position that indicates that she is willing and able to be mounted. Most female cats, even after neutering, will happily arch their backs when stroked but then so will many males too. A few females, after a short period of heavy stroking or a long period of gentling, may then flatten themselves onto the chair or floor and adopt the mating position, especially, of course, those which are about to call, or which have been mated before and treat the stroking as a form of foreplay. So, in some senses, Anna is indeed viewing her owners as potential mates and responding sexually to their attentions, and she is quite likely to continue to do so to some degree even after she has been spayed. But then they should call her sensual and affectionate rather than worry about any true sexual aspirations of her flirtatious behaviour.

NEITHER ONE THING NOR THE OTHER

Dear Mr Neville

Our two-year-old German Shepherd Dog, Rambo, is a

male, in the sense that he has a penis, but asexual in the fact that he has no testicles and squats to urinate like a bitch rather than lifting his leg. As he's always been very puppyish, we had hoped that he was just a late maturer but following an operation to see if his testicles were retained in his abdomen, our vet has informed us that Rambo has no testicles at all. What we would like to know is whether he will ever cock his leg and become more male in spite of this, or will he always be as he is now, neither one thing nor the other?

Yours sincerely

Carrie and Frank Eckington

The rather inappropriately named Rambo is included in this section to show just how much secondary sexual development in terms of character and behaviour comes under the control of the male hormone, testosterone, in our male dogs. Poor Rambo was the second anorchid (literally meaning 'having no testicles') dog that I have encountered in my practice, the other being a very sweet ten-year-old collie cross. They were similar in temperament, lacking any competitive drive, and were totally and innocently sweet natured. They were perpetual juveniles in their willingness to play and, being easily distracted when being trained, were something of an excitable handful on occasion though at least they were non-aggressive with their owners or other dogs. Though both had a functioning penis, neither ever cocked their leg, as this behaviour enables the adult male to scent mark territory while urinating, largely a male trait and one brought on by testosterone. As neither dog had any testes, neither produced any testosterone (not quite true, as some male hormone is produced by their adrenal glands, but in small quantities, probably not enough to fuel the secondary sexual advance) and so they would remain effectively as big pups all their lives. While both were friendly dogs, Rambo did demonstrate that testosterone doesn't affect either predatory or territorial defence aggression: he would give the postman hell every morning and chase with a vengeance any bird, cat, squirrel or rabbit that ever had the misfortune to cross his path.

WELL HELLO?

Dear Mr Neville

Our young Springer Spaniel, Ringo, has recently decided that the way to greet everyone is to stick his head firmly between their legs and thrust his nose upwards, while rudely snorting in a good draft of air. I realise that at a year and a bit, he is growing up and will now be far more aware of scents, particularly from that region of the body. But his behaviour is especially annoying and embarrassing when he does it to ladies; at its worst in the morning with a cold nose under a short bath robe when it is cold and painful! I've tried telling him off but to no avail . . . so how do I stop him?

Yours sincerely

Terry Golding

'Oh don't mind him, he's just saying hello!' How many times has that happened to me and, come to think of it, how many times did I say it to the uncomfortable victims of my Large Munsterlander's greeting before I actually set about practising what I preach and taught him not to. The 'nose between the legs and lift' greeting is a particular favourite of the medium to large size dog, usually a male

and of those breeds which have been specially selected for having a good nose. That usually means it will be an active and often forthright spaniel, labrador, retriever or Large Munsterlander or other of the gun dog breeds that snuffle between one's legs (to find out exactly what your status is today). Mind you, there's plenty a snipey-nosed Dobermann or German Shepherd that will give you the same friendly hello, and one must at least be grateful that hairier and often grubbier Shih Tzus, Lhasa Apsos and Pekingese can't reach that high, even with a child! For the dog, it's all very natural to head for an area where there's lots of scent information to be gleaned, it's like shaking hands in a world that we have so little sensory awareness of.

It's always pointless punishing dogs and cats for not behaving as we would like them to, but especially so when they do things which are natural for them, no matter how rude they may be for us. For dogs like Ringo, adolescence is the age when scents, and particularly sexual or personal scents, are taking on new social meanings and so this interest must be shaped and directed into areas that we find less of a problem. A dog with a good nose should ideally have opportunity to work with it in following trails or, easier for the average pet owner to organise, simple games of 'hunting the cheese' in the home and garden.

In treating the unwanted personal greetings, it's important to deter the dog subtly from what he is doing. A short squirt from a very unpleasant, but totally harmless and non-toxic bitter-tasting spray, such as the appropriately named 'Down Dog' or 'Bitter Apple' spray, from a small pump spray plastic bottle concealed in the hand, and applied as surreptitiously as possible to Ringo's mouth, will give a negative pay-off to his rude advances. The more surreptitious the spray, the more the dog will associate it with his initiating nosey behaviour rather than any response threat from the owner, and the more effective it will be. As the sprayed dog backs away a little, Terry should immediately encourage him to stay near him, sit on request and then receive the greeting that Terry wants to offer of a few kind words and a gentle stroke.

After just a few such experiences, Ringo will soon learn that when he meets people, he approaches gently and sits to receive their attentions, and that scenting them is not part of the greeting protocol. It usually works very quickly with a young dog and after only one or two harmless bitter-tasting thwarted lunges at the human groin, provided, of course, that the spray bottle is kept invisible, never used as a weapon or a threat and is associated by the dog with his actions and not as a challenge from his owner. It doesn't work any better for using a more offensive liquid or by aiming the foul-tasting liquid anywhere other than at the dog's mouth. It's equally important that the owner or person takes the time to teach the dog not to use canine introductions and at the same time help him to realise that greeting using human manners brings the desired rewards of friendship and contact. And then Terry, like me, after months of hanging on to my dog to keep his nose out of various guests' groins and passing it off with embarrassed remarks like, 'I really honestly didn't teach him to do that,' can relax knowing that his dog knows how to say hello without being sexually explicit.

BENDING OVER BACKWARDS TO HELP!

Dear Mr Neville

I am the very proud owner of an Anatolian Karabash, who is very large and already weighs well over 100 lb at eight months old, and who is also already very male! As well as being an almost perpetual flasher, he never misses an opportunity to try to mount me. Fortunately I am a big chap myself and can usually keep him down but unfortunately I also suffer from a bad back. If Turk can get me when I'm slightly off balance or half bent over, such as when I'm preparing vegetables or washing up at the sink, I just can't move quickly enough to get him off my back without causing myself serious pain. It's now become almost a game to Turk and I am very careful not to turn my back on him. My vet has advised me to have him castrated but I'm loath to do this as he is of rather a rare breed in this country and I had hoped to use him for breeding with my sister's bitch. Is there a safe way of living with him and is there any chance that he'll grow out of trying to jump on me every time he gets the chance?

Yours sorely

Robert Torrington

Ah well, what's a dog to do when he's only got a pack of one male to experiment with! Obviously all of Turk's experiments got directed towards his owner and, being a large dog, he usually got his way once he'd learned when he could take full advantage. Doubtless, Robert's bad back forced him to collapse slightly if caught unawares, and this perhaps indicated willingness to mate on the part of the inexperienced Turk. 'What on earth do you do when he pins you down?' I asked Robert during our consultation. He laughed a little nervously, as despite everything, he didn't want to risk me suggesting that Turk be castrated as the only solution to his problems. 'Wait till he's finished,' he laughed, 'and wriggle to speed him up!' When we'd stopped laughing, we settled on the safer policy of an anti-male hormone injection for Turk, and plenty of opportunity to meet bitches while his hormone-inspired sexuality was suppressed so that he could be the stud that Robert wanted him to be when he was mentally as advanced as he was sexually. The injection, incidentally, does reduce fertility for up to about six months, but doesn't make the dog actually infertile for long, if at all, so it's a great treatment for all male dogs of stud potential who cause their owners some grief while they're growing up. The manufacturers would, I'm sure, be delighted to know that their product meant no more faking for Robert, for a while anyway, and that he was extremely grateful for it!

FELINE FEELINGS

Dear Mr Neville

My young male cat Barnaby, who is only four and a half months old, has recently started to mount my arm whenever I am sat in the armchair watching television. Not only this, but he also makes some appalling wailing noises while he's doing it and bites my hand quite hard. He also gets quite nasty if I try to pull or shake him off, so now I keep a water pistol next to the chair to deter him. He only does this to me and not to anyone else in the family and only when I'm sitting in an armchair. He sleeps quite happily on my bed for much of the night and never attempts any such dastardly behaviour. Is it time to have him doctored? He's about six months old.

Yours sincerely

Eric Sidwell

As we saw with Anna, Mr and Mrs Smith's young female cat, the onset of adolescence brings sexual drives to the fore with some individuals, and a little earlier than one might normally expect. Some are quite demonstrative in their actions and can also be quite specific about when and where they 'perform' until they gain wider social experience with other cats, or they find themselves at the vet's to be neutered. Young male cats and some adults too, especially un-neutered toms of course, may grab the arms of their owners and mount them vigorously and with a fixed, slightly 'other-worldly' look in their eye. The behaviour is far less common than in young male dogs and usually occurs in response to the early surges of male hormone production. Assuming that the testicles have descended into the scrotum, it's a sure sign that the cat has entered puberty and that, as most owners usually demand, Barnaby and his ilk should be whipped off to the vet to have them whipped off in return. Such early sexual expression may indicate a rather macho male character is developing so perhaps Barnaby more than most would otherwise be likely to develop strong secondary male characteristics which are incompatible with rewarding pet keeping. These may include smelly pungent urine spraying, indoors as well as out, roaming in search of queens and to establish a large territory generally, and highly combative territorial fighting with other males. This can lead to frequent and large veterinary bills for patching up the wounded cat and lancing the abscesses that invariably develop in the wounds inflicted by other cats' claws when a direct hit is suffered. That's why male cats are castrated and usually before it all starts to happen, not in response to it.

Sexually the young male may grasp mountable inanimate objects, as we shall see in Chapter 7, but is far more likely to be turned on by a live target. For the majority of cats, the most available living object is indeed their owner's arm, which they typically grab after a few moments of stroking and petting. This is probably viewed as nuzzling foreplay at such times by the cat, and is the type of contact that fires up the instinctive drives to respond to any early testosterone circulating through his body. The painful grab is the typical mating reaction of a tom cat, who would grab the scruff of the queen to pin her down during coitus, and all the noise that Barnaby is making is just because 'cats do it noisily'. As with most animals, ourselves included, any form of arousal or excitement can easily trip into aggression if we are challenged or upset, so Eric is indeed wise to use a water pistol when Barnaby is feeling fruity and not his free hand to pull him off. But better for all would be not to excite Barnaby in the first place with too long or too intense a period of stroking and to pay a visit with him to the vet without delay.

A LOAD OF BULL?

Dear Mr Neville

A strange change has come over my Basset Fauve de Bretagnes dog, Bolter, since last weekend. Until then he was a fairly quiet if quite stubborn character, but one who would generally do what he was asked to. He's about a year and a half old but although he's about fully grown and obviously mature sexually, he's never demonstrated any sexual behaviour, until now. Last weekend we took him to our cottage in the countryside and paid a visit to my cousin's farm. By coincidence, the vet was there converting all the seven-week-old bull calves into bullocks out in the main field. As he castrated them by removing their testes, Bolter lived up his name and wolfed them down, still warm. The vet said it wouldn't do him any harm and that it was nice to see the products of his labours going to good use for once! As Bolter had managed to chomp his way through about twenty-five pairs of fresh meat balls, he suggested that we'd probably saved ourselves the cost of feeding him that night!

We arrived back home on the evening of the following day with Bolter asleep in the car all the way, clearly tired from his weekend charging around the countryside and helping the vet. But when he woke up on the Monday morning, he was clearly a very different dog to the one we'd known before. He'd become very 'strutty', growled at the cats, growled at us when we told him to get out of his basket to go into the garden, cocked his leg over just about every bush we own and then came back inside and cocked his leg up the kitchen table leg. Astounded by this 'Jekyll and Hyde' change, I put his lead on to take him for his usual morning walk in the local park a bit earlier than usual. We were no sooner inside the gate than he picked a fight with a male black Labrador who was minding his own business, picked a second fight with a small Terrier and then tried to mount a German Shepherd bitch without so much as a 'by your leave'. She snapped at him, but he persisted until I pulled him off and brought him straight home in disgrace. As well as all this macho male behaviour that's gone on since the weekend, we're also sure that his facial hair is growing thicker and longer . . . or are we imagining things?

He seems to be getting back to his normal quieter self now, a week on from our trip to the farm so we can only presume that, through eating all those bull bits, he had a 'hormone high' and has been responding to it ever since. Could this really happen or could Bolter have been responding to something else? Is there anything we should be careful of long term?

Yours sincerely

Caroline and Derek Penrose

Good old Bolter! He is the only example of his rather rare breed that I have ever seen and could be best described, with the nicest of intentions, as a sort of coarse-coated delightfully scruffy thick-set Dachshund! He was growing up into a pleasant and easy-going dog, with no problems of a 'male' kind reported by Caroline and Derek until the incident with the calves occurred. On checking with my veterinary colleagues, it appeared that what had happened to Bolter was indeed possible and that even testosterone from a different species could be expected to have an effect. Testosterone and many other hormones can be taken orally and can be absorbed into the bloodstream without being broken down, in fact there are several commercial hormone preparations which can be given orally or by injection and which have fairly fast-acting effects. But before you rush off to have your slow-to-develop young male dog or reluctant stud jabbed full of bovine testosterone, it's worth pointing out that vets would be most unlikely to offer him any without genuine medical need, and nor would a GP be likely to offer such treatment to any man in need of a quick pick-me-up . . . so it's back to the raw sweetbreads from the butcher, I'm afraid!

Poor Bolter, unwittingly, could have received a huge testosterone surge from consuming what he did and once in his bloodstream, this would be highly likely to alter his behaviour in the manner observed. The only question was whether the calves' testicles would have contained much testosterone as they were rather underdeveloped, their owners being aged about eight weeks at the time of their castration. Clearly from Bolter's response, there was enough hormone in the volume he consumed to cause an effect or, at least, to build upon his own adolescent testosterone surges and cause some physical changes as well. Fortunately, after a few days of being unbearably aggressively macho, he returned to his normal trouble-free adolescent self and a life of being sociable to other dogs and friendly without being overly amorous to the bitches in his local park. For Bolter, this was indeed a Jekyll and Hyde experience which brought home to me just how much of an effect testosterone can have on a normally placid dog's behaviour and just how much of a shock this can be to the owners, if not the dog, when that testosterone is produced by the dog himself and not introduced from such a readily identifiable outside source. The experience ensured that Bolter never again went to the farm at calf (or pig or lamb) castrating time and was never fed anything other than his usual complete dry dog food, at least until he grew up. And, I'm delighted to say, Bolter has remained a perfect Dr Jekyll, with no resurgence of Mr Hyde and as the activity of his own testicles have never once given cause for concern, they remain firmly attached to him.

THE INSURMOUNTABLE CAT

Dear Mr Neville

Scruff, my eighteen-month-old Jack Russell lives a quiet life with me and my tortoiseshell long-haired cat, Puddles, who is a neutered male. In recent months, Scruff seems to have developed a strange obsession about Puddles, following him around the flat and constantly trying to mount him. After a couple of close shaves requiring a paw of claws to dissuade Scruff, Puddles now sleeps on shelves or on the fridge and well out of range of his advances. Is Scruff just over-sexed or does he just fancy what is, after all, a very beautiful cat for some reason best known to himself?

Yours truly

Veronica Thornton

The young male dog does what comes instinctively into his mind when sexually aroused. In the absence of other dogs, or even his litter mates to experiment with, he may mount any grippable objects or creatures that he can find. We'll

look at some of the bizarre inanimate objects that dogs choose to experiment with in Chapter 7, but you can imagine the surprise on the face of Puddles when Scruff suddenly decided to take a fancy to him. Unlike the reverse case of Monty the cat (see page 184), Scruff is not responding to any cues from Puddles other than his physical presence. He is simply responding to his own drives and, being aware enough socially to know that he shouldn't attempt to mount his owner and in the absence of any canine opportunity, the cat is a better proposition than anything else accessible. Enlightening for the cat and surprising for Veronica, but rather sad for the highly social Scruff, caught up in a world without enough dogs in it for him to learn how to grow up. For sure the remedy here is to get him out more and for him to meet lots of other dogs in the park even if Veronica, like many owners, would probably find more than one dog too much to cope with at home. It's a case of Veronica understanding Scruff's social and developmental needs and trying to compensate for the fact that he encounters so few of his own kind in his life as a pet. It's an approach that I am commonly urging dog owners especially to adopt with a range of behaviour problems that are referred to me and not just in those concerning adolescents with obvious physical or social difficulties in expressing their developing sexuality in a human world. It's just that with adolescent anythings, sex is very high on the list of new things to be experimented with and developed in a social context but then that, I believe, is the point of the whole process. It's a point we all too often forget or only notice when it causes us embarrassment as the cases in this chapter have demonstrated.

In the next two chapters we'll take a closer look at how we influence and control the sexual lives and opportunities of our pets and how our own behaviour can sometimes be affected to bizarre levels as a result of our own misconceptions, as well as those of our cats and dogs.

4
Sexual Confusions in the Human Pack

'Those who restrain desire do so because theirs is weak enough to be restrained' WILLIAM BLAKE

We humans are lucky to have evolved to such an advanced state that we live much of our lives without considering our survival at every moment of the day, are able to control our living environment and to have developed such a level of self-awareness. We enjoy a life that is far removed from one where sex is purely to reproduce ourselves, and enjoy the mating process as an emotional as well as a physical experience. There are three types of sex that human beings engage in: junk food sex which is usually a one-off occasion with an unfamiliar partner; snack sex, where the relationship is casual and impermanent; and the three-course meal version based on a close emotional and usually exclusive relationship, often cemented by marriage and the production of children. The physical sex within any of these three types can be fun and fulfilling even if the level of emotional commitment varies from none to total.

With animals, it seems that most engage in sex simply for the purposes of procreation, and have only what in human terms would be regarded as junk food or snack sex. Three-course meals are not on the menu because successful procreation doesn't usually demand a close emotional relationship to exist between the parents even if the relationship can sometimes take the form of a lifelong pairbond. Sex is short and sweet, even if courtship may take some time, unless you're a pair of hippopotami, which often mate for up to two hours and more, or stick insects, which have been known to couple for seventy-nine days, or pythons, who may mate for one hundred and eighty days! Of course, junk food sex may be oft repeated within a period of mating, as with desert rats which may couple as often as one hundred and twenty times in an hour. Phew!

Despite this, animals don't appear to enjoy sex for it's own sake . . . or do they? Can we really pretend that there isn't a glint in the male dog's eye? Perhaps it's less obvious in the tom cat, but can we be absolutely sure that our pets have no emotional appreciation when having sex? Is it purely a functional affair? Or is it just that we don't recognise the signs of enjoyment that they're giving off? For enjoyment, one might just as easily read 'emotional fulfilment'. It's a concept that must surely be more relevant to a creature higher up the evolutionary scale with correspondingly greater internal and external awareness, such as a hippo, than for an insect. Fulfilment may simply mean a feeling of positive feedback for the individual at having located and mated with another of the opposite sex, and thereafter it's a case of getting on with surviving until driven to the next opportunity. There must be a positive feedback from the process simply because if the feelings were negative, animals with a sense of self-awareness might otherwise override the innate desire to reproduce. In other words, the body could choose to ignore the genes. The Praying Mantis female chews off her partner's head during copulation so one must presume that he has no idea that such a fate lies ahead for him as he looks for a mate, or it wouldn't take much emotional complexity to decide to be celibate. And what's the last thing to pass through the mind of a mating male Praying Mantis? His mate's jaws!

There does seem to be some emotional fulfilment derived from the mating process in the cat. Courtship, though dictated largely by the receptivity of the queen, still involves much friendly interplay and the evidence of foreplay involving licking, touching and bodily rubbing surely indicates enjoyment of the process as cats engage in this type of social physical contact purely for the pleasure it brings at other times than when mating. But although this friendly physical contact occurs very much at the time of mating, the actual mating process between tom and queen is nonetheless usually a short affair. After mating, the tom clears off in search of another opportunity to spread his genes and the queen is left to care for herself and her kittens without the benefit of any lasting social, physical or emotional relationship with her mate. The survival chances of the kittens depend entirely on their mother's emotional bond to them and physical ability to care for them and, other than at mating time, this will be the only time in their lives when their chance of survival demands that they communicate their emotional state, such as hunger, distress, cold, etc., to another member of their species.

Animals that have evolved to live in groups need to communicate with one another in order to survive, otherwise they might as well be more solitary like the cat. Communication is the art of letting other social contacts know how you are feeling, what you are intending and what your response is to their actions. For it to work, the system requires that all involved have a well-developed ability to receive information and respond accordingly. In social insects such as bees and ants, this is apparently achieved chemically and through specific members of the group being produced to fulfil only a limited range of tasks: worker or queen, for example. Complex, reactive and intelligent mammals such as dogs and people need a greater level of emotional awareness to be successful because the response of individuals is far more important within the social group. It's the nature and strength of the relationship between a breeding pair that starts to count in the fulfilment of the demands of the drives dictated by their genes.

Wolves and wild dogs such as Jackals, Coyotes and African Hunting Dogs form strong bonds between the breeding pairs to ensure that their fitness is passed to the next generation within the protection afforded by their pack. But this simply couldn't happen if they couldn't communicate their high status to their pack mates, nor if the top bitch and top male didn't get on. It's easy to presume that the drive to procreate overrides their emotions as individuals and that it doesn't matter whether the dog and bitch like each other or not. But it doesn't take too much emotion to creep into the observations made by ethologists to see that any successful top breeding pair do enjoy each other's company and spend a lot of time together without constantly pursuing the demands of their genes. The act of sex itself may be brief, perhaps of the junk food or snack variety with no earth-moving three-course meals, but clearly there is an emotional bond between them and I would suggest that if there wasn't, they wouldn't be able to enjoy having a stable pack around them. In this case, either other dogs would come to front the hierarchy and have the chance to establish the right to breed, or the group would dissolve into smaller units and wander away to encounter other small units to bond up with and form a new breeding pack.

In short, as with humans, I am suggesting that the emotional bond between the parents is as vital to the success of their attempts to breed and to the ultimate security and survival of their offspring within the family unit as is the strength of their individual characteristics that have brought them the opportunity to breed. After all, an individual bitch could be extremely strong and become the highest ranking female in the group, but if that threw her into a breeding relationship with the equally fit-to-breed top male but they were unable to form a pair bond because they had always squabbled and kept distant from each other in the group, then they are unlikely to make successful parents. Naturally, many other influences are at play in this complex canine society, such as the age of the two individuals and their experience and ability to communicate their intentions and emotions. The size, age and social cohesion of their pack will also play a vital role in their success. A long-established stable pack, much like long-established human societies, will usually provide the best social opportunity for the 'right' pair to come together, but the pack will also be able to adjust, perhaps fragment a little, and allow others to come through if that pair can't bond closely enough in order to protect the success of the common genetic component to be found in all members.

It's an arrangement that is similar to the tribal system of older human cultures (and more so than the one of technological western man) but this, too, is logical — after all, dog and man are both social mammals. It's certainly logical to presume that emotional bonding is playing an important role in the whole process of mate selection and reproduction in a creature as intensely social as the dog, even if we have great difficulty in recognising the fine subtleties of the communication of those emotions between dogs or wolves in a pack. Of course, many scientists have also been rather block-headed in their outlook when studying such matters and arrogantly presumed that because they can't see emotion, it can't be quantified and therefore doesn't exist. The same scientists will then go home to their pet dogs and see and happily describe a whole range of emotions and mood changes in them!

With dogs' wild cousins, as it was with their ancestors, sexual behaviour may be governed by social disciplines, but relations for the pet dog in the human pack are so altered that those disciplines are now often confused or lost and are certainly not replaced by human-style moral awareness. There thus is little social control on our pet's sexual behaviour other than the human kind which comes in response to it when it appears. The emotional shallowness of the sex then before us is what we expect from a 'lesser' creature, but lacking higher emotions it is impossible for a cat or a dog to develop morals about any issue and readjust its behaviour to fit into our social herd. It's hard enough for a dog to know where and how to fit in, given so many confusing signals, but especially difficult with regard to sex, the behaviour that has more moral codes attached to it than any other aspect of our lives. The lack of emotional perception also fuels our protective and nurturing feelings towards our pets in the same way as it does in our children, but we perhaps inadvertently expect them all to develop a moral sense in time. Our pets, of course, never do, but we only have to face that reality when they face us with sex in their minds.

In spite of the success it has achieved as a result of becoming a pet, the absorption of the dog into the human tribe can lead to so many problems for it. The total number of pack members required for stability is far reduced compared with a wolf, wild dog or even feral dog pack and so the natural canine constraints and mechanisms that decide who should breed in the pack are lost. As a result of this, and through some of the commoner general effects of breeding for domestication, the pet dog is far more promiscuous than his ancestors or cousins and will happily engage in junk food sex given the slightest opportunity. Some of this willingness arises because puppies usually lose contact with their early canine companions at about eight or ten weeks of age, before they have reached emotional or physical maturity and are only just capable of an independent nutritional existence. They may be young and capable of adapting to life in their human pack, but so many of the social rules they've relied on up to now are suddenly changed. The 'natural' constraints of purely canine development are lost or watered down and there is greatly restricted opportunity to learn how to be a dog in a pack. Instead this is replaced by the opportunity for the young dog later to meet unrelated and unfamiliar dogs and so is also bound to scramble some of its normal socio-sexual developmental pathways.

As a result of this more liberal period of upbringing, as we have seen in earlier chapters, male dogs will usually wander away from their human pack in response to the dictates of their own hormones or the whiff of a bitch in season and try to mate, never having seen the bitch before and with no intention of hanging around afterwards as he would in a cohesive dog pack. There is also simply no prospect of a paternal role for the male pet dog because there is no pack for him to play it out in. The bitch alone, or her owners, now ensures the success of the species and she no longer requires him for anything other than his sperm.

However, he continues to function and behave as he would in a dog pack back in his own home. And this can lead to great problems for his human owners if he perceives himself as having the right to mate within the group when he clearly lacks the opportunity. Inadvertently, we can often give an otherwise low or middle ranking male dog the idea that he has achieved sufficiently high status within our social set-up to dictate our actions and to look for a mate simply because we have failed to understand the mechanisms of social organisation that he has evolved to respond to. My clinics are full of dogs with such unearned high views of themselves and which are behaving naturally according to their own dictates but which, in the human pack, have caused great upset and with behaviours ranging from lack of control to biting aggression and overt displays of sexual behaviour towards their owners. But, while such problems could arise in almost any family dog, given the human way that we assimilate them into our social packs, the root cause of most 'straight' sexual problems in some of our young male dogs arises from a simple lack of opportunity for them to grow up as dogs within the human pack.

GOD'S MAN PLAYED

'Did you know . . . there are three sexes — men, women and clergymen?' REVD SYDNEY SMITH

Dear Mr Neville

I write to you in total desperation and hope that you will be able to help me. I am sure that you will understand the need for your utmost confidence when I say that my dog, Rusty, a two-year-old Irish Setter, seems to have a fixation about our local vicar. He is a frequent caller to my house as we work closely organising tea parties, coffee mornings and other events in aid of our village church. Rusty has always liked him from puppyhood and until last weekend was content to go mad with delight when he first arrives but then sit calmly next to him as we talk and gaze at him with loving eyes. The Reverend Catchpole, though not at all what you might call 'an animal person', is, however, as you would expect, a very kind man and would pat Rusty a little and even 'accidentally' drop an occasional biscuit for him. You can imagine his and our surprise, not to mention acute embarrassment, when last weekend Rusty sidled up to the vicar in my garden and, after receiving a customary stroke, proceeded to mount his leg furiously. While this would have been bad enough in my lounge, alas this occurred outside on my lawn during a Women's Institute garden party. The poor man was absolutely mortified and didn't know what to do. Rusty's grip was extremely strong and he simply couldn't shake him off and eventually it took four or five of our members to dislodge him, which involved no little manhandling of dog and vicar. I'm so ashamed, and though the vicar has overcome his embarrassment, I'm anxious that Rusty never again behaves so monstrously with him or anyone else. Why would he have done this? He certainly isn't a sexy dog at all with me or my husband and apart from being a little scatty like most of his breed, he's normally well behaved and very pleasant to keep.

Yours sincerely

Mavis Lyons

From his owner's point of view, even allowing for the excitability of his breed, Rusty was the perfect pet dog prior to this assault on a man of the cloth. Friendly, a good guard, well-mannered with guests after he'd settled down from an initial welcome, a part of home and family and, most importantly, to all intents and purposes, asexual. From Rusty's point of view, he's well assimilated into life in the human pack, he's learnt how to communicate when he wants something and many of his natural reactions, such as barking when there's a knock at the door, are encouraged. He happily welcomes his pack leaders' visitors as temporary members of the group in the den after he's seen that his pack leaders are friendly and accepting of them. But his natural social drives also tell him that the more frequent and well received the visitor, the more he or she is to be viewed as part of the family and the closer the bond that he forms with them will be.

For Rusty, the young male dog, now is the age at which to start forming close relations with individuals within the group. Typically in a dog or wolf pack, he would form a coalition or 'gang' with other males of around the same age, particularly his brothers. They would spend much time together, learn how to hunt and continue learning how to socialise between themselves. They may also practise sexual postures such as mounting each other, both as part of defining their own inter-relations and in developing the necessary preliminary physical skills for mating later. This type of behaviour usually then becomes applied with a more direct sexual connotation towards young bitches in the group, who will have gone through a similar, though less overtly competitive learning phase themselves in a coalition of young females. Of course, the two sexes and all ages interact constantly but an analysis of the amount of time each dog spends with others in the group often reveals this type of temporary gang for both sexes, which functions as a sort of safe platform to develop more individual relationships with the opposite sex as the dogs grow up. Any young dog may also establish a close pair bond with another of either sex, though perhaps initially one of the same sex from within the 'gang'. The pair will spend much time together playing, hunter-scavenging or just lying close by until such time as they become more adult, when a greater variety of relationships develop and they themselves may be called upon to play 'auntie' or 'uncle' in helping their parents raise the latest litter of their brothers and sisters.

It's all very similar, of course, to what happens in human society across a great range of cultures and so can be presumed to be a system of emotional and social development that evolved in social mammals for good reason. The pair bond is also the reason why some dogs can form extraordinarily close attachments to one person. Though this is more likely when they are kept by single owners it can occur even when the dog is raised in a family situation and, sometimes, even when the dog gets to meet enormous numbers of people and other dogs and ought to 'grow out' of the pair bond and be able to spread its loyalties around more. This can be very frustrating for the members of the family who aren't favoured and who gaze bemused, and often enviously, at the human side of the pair, wondering what it is that their relation has that they lack for the dog to love them so. It's even more annoying when, as I am commonly presented with at my clinics, a bitch that is fed, walked and cared for by the wife and kids all day simply sits and waits by the door or sulks in her bed waiting for the husband to come home from work. Then she abandons any small thoughts of her daytime companions to follow him and sit close to him at every opportunity, lovingly gazing at her hero, who may do absolutely nothing in terms of feeding, walking or caring for her.

Pair bonding can arise between any pair of young dogs or between any dog/human pair, though it does seem to occur more commonly between a human and a dog of the opposite sex in the human pack. But whatever the structure of this often frustrating bond, while the lucky human of the pair regards it as a close act of friendship and loyalty from the dog, in canine terms the relationship could theoretically be regarded as one 'trapped in time' if the bonding is so strong that the dog fails to relate to any other person or dog at home as it becomes adult. Ordinarily, one would expect such a close pair bond to have dissolved slowly into multi-lateral friendship with everyone by the time the dog has reached two and a half to three years of age.

But back to Rusty, whose drives have been telling him for about a year to get into a gang and pair bond, though it's never really been possible with his owners, a pack of one middle-aged man and one middle-aged woman. Instead, much of his social learning has been directed towards non-immediate members of the pack, through infrequent social encounters in the park with other dogs and through meeting his pack leaders' human friends, both at home and outside. This usually keeps a dog's social abilities and friend-recognition systems ideally spread to make a sociable and friendly pet that fits easily into human society but can often deny him the opportunity to grow up socio-sexually as a dog. This is not usually a recognisable problem for the owners, who invariably wouldn't want a 'socio-sexually mature dog' anyway. For Rusty, and the other occasionally strongly motivated individual, the need to form a pair bond with a pack mate persists despite human demands or restrictions. Having viewed the Reverend Catchpole increasingly as a pack member from their frequent encounters, Rusty probably came to regard him making up his somewhat truncated male gang. Then, later into adolescence and with strong social suppression from his owners and a lack of opportunity denying any other form of socio-sexual experimentation, Rusty's frustrations exploded into action at the garden party. Doubtless already excited by the sudden surge in the size of his pack and greatly improved social opportunities for the afternoon, Rusty's desire to experiment naturally focused most on the security of his gang-mate, the vicar, and with the observed rather ungodly results.

Poor Mavis, who was unable to move comfortably in her own human social world for some time after Rusty's performance, was at least reassured by the information that Rusty would probably grow out of his infatuation, and develop a more controlled, friendly and adult relationship with the Reverend Catchpole as he grew up and completely out of the 'gang' phase. However, I did point out quite clearly that this would only be the case if Rusty was given plenty of increased opportunity to meet other dogs. In this case, I also suggested that as Rusty then generally led a rather quiet life, it may be wiser to get another dog with whom he could focus his canine social developments a little more safely, providing Mavis and her husband could cope with having a small pack around the place. It was one of the few cases where another male dog would usually be as good an idea as getting a bitch, though this was due to the fact that Rusty was a very friendly dog who wasn't competitive with other males and who could be expected to organise a peaceful friendly hierarchy and be just as happy being number one dog or number two.

This case differs from problems concerning overtly sexual and competitive males for whom the addition of another male to the pack presents a challenge to be tackled and for whom the companionship of a bitch is a far better social prospect, with suitable attention paid to birth control of course. And I was right, though I strongly suspect that tales of how the Reverend Catchpole was defended from a devil-inspired canine sex pervert by a gang of old ladies armed with handbags at a Women's Institute garden party resounded hilariously in the village pub for years afterwards!

NO KIDDING!

Dear Mr Neville

My husband and I delayed starting a family until we had moved out of London to the countryside, but fulfilled some of our nurturing ambitions by keeping Bessie, a beautiful Flat-coated Retriever. I'd admit that she's been spoiled by being the only 'baby' with regular walks in Hyde Park and the best of everything and revelled as much as we did in the fields and space of our new home. She took the arrival of our son, Justin, quite well, considering that she then had competition for our affections and some areas of the house, such as his bedroom, became 'no-go' areas for her. Justin has always been very affectionate towards Bessie and, like most children, he wants to follow her and pat her. We've always been careful to supervise their interactions and to try and teach Justin to be gentle when he touches Bessie. In fact we had no problems at all between them when Justin started to walk. Now, on a couple of occasions when they've been playing together, Bessie has growled quite fiercely at him when he's put his arms around her to cuddle her. We're a little puzzled by this, as Bessie tolerates far worse mauling around and even enjoys his rough attentions at all other times. But when he throws his arms around her neck, she stiffens, raises her neck and head and gives a nasty growl that rises in anger the longer he holds on. Of course Justin, at three years of age, has not yet learned that the growl means 'back off' and so we are still having to be very careful about letting them play together when we'd hoped that we could be more relaxed by now. Why is it that Bessie doesn't appreciate this type of handling from Justin when she happily accepts it from my husband and myself or any other adult? Is Justin likely to be bitten if we accidentally lapse in our supervision?

Yours sincerely

Amanda Golding

The communication gap between man and dog is always likely to be at its greatest when young children are involved. After all, if they are still learning to communicate with human language, one can hardly expect them to speak 'dog'. Amanda and her husband have carefully done what all responsible parents do when the babies arrive in a family with a dog in it. They've established safe areas and supervised all the interactions between child and dog from day one. When the baby is still tiny and unable to crawl or toddle, most dogs actually benefit enormously from their presence. It means more chance of contact with other members of the pack, in fact probably permanent company with the mother if, prior to starting a family, she has been away from home during the day pursuing a career. Having a baby join the pack usually means more walks 'en famille', the prospect of lots of dropped titbits to be slurped up under the high chair after the baby starts to take solid food and very little change for the worse in the nature of social relations that the dog enjoys with the adult owners. Problems usually only start to occur once the baby has grown up enough to start to crawl. Then parents must supervise things carefully if the new exploratory rug-rat is not to make the dog's life hell with constant chasing and cornering in areas that the dog used to regard as safe, quiet resting areas under the table or in a favourite corner or bed.

The majority of cases I get to see involving children and dogs are referred because a previously good-natured dog, which has never so much as growled at anyone, has been forced into making a growl or even given a warning snap bite to an unsupervised child that has chased it into a corner and started poking, prodding or pulling hair and given it no chance of escape. The fault lies not with the dog, indeed, prior to any growl or bite, it has usually given all reasonable forms of threat or submissive reactions designed in doggy language to ask the child to back away.

Of course, it's not the child's fault either that he or she keeps pursuing the annoyed or frightened dog, especially when the reaction of the dog is so interesting. The fault lies clearly with the parents or nanny or childminder for not having supervised the dog and child or safely separated them to play or rest on their own. It's all too easy to blame the dog and just expect it to tolerate all manner of social abuse from the newly mobile child but if, like me, you are the parent of a very inquisitive, very wriggly and highly social eighteen-month-old you'll know that it's very often the case that it's the dog that needs protecting from the child rather than vice versa!

Amanda and her husband do seem to have done everything very responsibly and very carefully and, until Justin could actually stand and walk, have had no problems with the affable and easy-going Bessie. And this in spite of the fact that they admit to having spoiled her and treated her as something of a child substitute and allowed her lots of unearned social privileges prior to the arrival of their son. So why the problem now and of such a restricted nature? The answer is simple and sexual. Bessie will tolerate all manner of rough handling from the young Justin except when he clasps her around the neck and shoulders because this behaviour mimics the first stage of mounting. While Bessie will accept that her higher-ranking adult owners have the right to attempt to mount her in a social, or even sexual context if they so wish and won't growl at them, the young Justin simply hasn't gained sufficient standing in her pack to be able to take such liberties, sexual or social. Until now she has regarded him as a puppy produced by the breeding pair of her pack and has played 'auntie' as far as she has been allowed in bringing him up. She has tolerated his rough and clumsy play and endured some disruption without protest because she viewed him as a non-competitive junior member of the group.

Unbeknown to him, Justin is now mimicking the action of a young adolescent male dog of the equivalent age of a thirteen-year-old boy, not a three-year-old, and Bessie is disciplining him in the same way when he attempts to mount. First a stare, perhaps, then a stiffening of the body and a low growl deepening in tone if Justin fails to get the message and let go. At this age, of course, he won't get the message and Bessie's next action may well indeed be a snap bark or a snap bite. The bite will be designed to miss and be intended simply to frighten, but sadly the aim may not be so precise as intended or the child may move suddenly as it is delivered and may receive a painful nip on the face or hands. The snap bark or mock bite, and certainly an intended bite will usually achieve the desired effect on the child and make him let go, though in all too many cases, this alone spells the end of the dog's life as the understandably worried parents whisk their 'dangerous' dog off to the vet to be put to sleep.

But the fault is theirs. The dog was behaving normally by warning the child not to take social liberties or take sexual advantage, but the child couldn't interpret the language. The only way for Amanda and her husband to avoid such risks and misunderstandings between Bessie and Justin is to continue to supervise all introductions and keep the two friends safely apart when they can't until they are sure that Justin is old enough to be taught how to handle and relate to Bessie with gentleness and respect. This must continue until Bessie has perceived him fully to be a higher-ranking member of her pack with the same concomitant rights of handling her where he wants and how he wants, which she accords her adult owners.

For dogs like Bessie, this perception may not develop until the child is perhaps six or seven years of age, by which time she will be needing a quieter life as an old dog anyway. It all depends on the individual dog, child, and parents, of course. There must be the opportunity for plenty of calm and supervised introductions but, as ever, if there is any doubt, the dog and child must never be left alone unsupervised whatever their ages or perceptions of status in the pack. At the end of the day it doesn't really matter if your child's behaviour is interpreted as a sexual

advance, a social indiscretion or an outright assault by the dog if he or she ends up with her face scarred for life and the dog ends up in a black plastic body bag. Both tragedies will, forever, remain the fault of the parents.

CYCLING ALONG WITH THE DOG

Dear Mr Neville

I have something of an embarrassing problem with my English Springer Spaniel, Merlin. Whenever I am having my period, but especially about twelve days afterwards when I am presumably ovulating, he gets extremely excited (even more than usual that is!) and won't leave me alone. He follows me around all day and whines and groans if I shut him in a different room, which I do just to get a bit of peace. If I sit down, he's constantly trying to shove his nose between my legs and paces up and down in front of me panting fast with horrible hot breath from his half-open mouth. He really is a disgusting letch and I find it acutely embarrassing to have anybody round to my house at this time. I'm also unable to take him for a walk because he simply won't leave me to go and run or chase his ball. Instead he pads along behind me drooling and waiting for the moment when I stop to talk to someone so that he can launch another of his horrible nasal attacks. My vet has advised me to have Merlin castrated but, as his problems seem entirely related to my cycle, this seems a bit unfair and, anyway, he reverts to normal shortly after my period has started and stays that way for a couple of weeks. Then then has a bad day or two and is fine again until a few days before my next period is due . . . and so it goes on! Are there any other options for us than to have him castrated and will it really make any difference to him?

Yours sincerely

Penelope Charles

One can't help but feel sorry for both Penelope and Merlin in this situation. Ordinarily they had the ideal owner/pet relationship where Merlin was thoroughly well looked after as the only dog. Although many of the rules that govern canine social society could be set aside by his owner's 'spoiling' of him in a human way, and accord him unearned privileges in the group, as with the vast majority of us, Penelope got away with it, to the greater enjoyment of both of them. Merlin simply revelled in being able to enjoy such a close relationship with his owner, sleeping in the bedroom, curling up with her on the couch in the evening and being fed all manner of tasty titbits on demand. He was never a pest, never disobedient and got on well with all other dogs in the park and with all of Penelope's many friends. It was the perfect pair bond. Merlin had been handed his top bitch on a plate and they both had a thoroughly good time.

When I met them both in Penelope's lovely house in the north-west of England, I wished, and not for the first time when treating my clients' dogs, that my own dogs were as little trouble and so much fun. Hiding her red face Penelope then started to tell me about her problem with the wonderful Merlin, but her blushes soon disappeared when I explained that Merlin was responding to perfectly understandable cues. Every month, as Penelope ovulated, she inadvertently gave off all the right chemical signals that said to her pair-bonded male dog, 'I am now available to mate.' And, as befits the highest-ranking male in the pack, even if it is by virtue of being the only one, he responded by showing the appropriate responses to the cues that evolution had prewired him to be sensitive to. He never went as far as attempting to mount his 'partner' because she had naturally never gone on to demonstrate her availability behaviourally and constantly rejected his interested nose. But, until the pheromones stopped flowing, in his own mind Merlin remained a dog with an open invitation, irrespective of how Penelope chose to reject him. In women, ovulation and menstruation are about half a month apart whereas the bitch ovulates while giving off a pheromone-laden discharge which is soon followed by menstruation if she is not mated. Hence poor Merlin found his owner of great sexual interest not only when she ovulated, but also to a slightly lesser degree when she actually started to menstruate, despite the hormone systems at play being slightly out of order from a dog's point of view. This was no reflection on Penelope, she could have changed her clothes and washed a thousand times per day but would never have been able to put Merlin off the scent. His nose is designed to detect one part of the appropriate pheromone in millions on the wind, so working out when his owner was of interest would be no problem! Quite why more women owners don't suffer with this problem in their male dogs is a mystery to me. Perhaps some give off far stronger pheromones than others, perhaps some dogs are more sensitive to human scent than others or perhaps, more likely, the majority of dogs actually sense the changes but have learnt to ignore the language of scent in their owners and other people as it is never otherwise used in their communications.

In this case, I agreed that it would be a pity if Merlin were to be castrated for this problem which, though it was a regular nuisance, only ever caused embarrassment for a few days and was never directed at any of Penelope's women friends at similar junctures of their sexual cycles, presumably because of the lack of any on-going pair bond with Merlin. It also seemed a pity to recommend any changes in their general lifestyle or living arrangements as Merlin and Penelope got along so perfectly. I was going to suggest that Merlin either be boarded with a friend or at his usual kennels for the few unbearably embarrassing days of problems or that his ardour was suppressed chemically every other period by the vet to give Penelope a break. But Penelope, now fully aware of the inevitability of the situation, solved the problem herself. 'I'll just have to go back on the pill so that my periods are lighter and hopefully less attractive for him, and perhaps stay on it for a few months at a time so that I stop having periods altogether for a while,' she said, 'though please don't tell anyone that it's for my dog, or people really will get the wrong idea!' And, despite medical advice to the contrary, she did, and I didn't and both their names are changed to be preserved in anonymity even now!

So, what with different social rules, differing forms of communication involving different senses and misinterpretations rife between man, woman and male dog on the sexual front, it's small wonder that the subject has caused us such difficulty in discussion. But while we can improve our understanding of canine socio-sexual behaviour and adjust our reactions to their sexual antics, what we can't do is make a fertile bitch behave as anything other than a fertile bitch in a pack. As we have seen, the cycle of the bitch in the human pack is not suppressed by the cycles of the top bitch as they may often be in a dog pack. This is partly because the closeness of the social relationship between woman and bitch takes a different form than between bitch and bitch, and partly because women's pheromones are presumably not exactly right in chemical terms to induce the appropriate physiological suppression required in the bitch's cycle. Additionally, we have altered the nature of reproductive cycles in the domestic dog to make them less sensitive to any outside influences with our artificial maintenance of temperature and light in the den. In domesticating the dog, and other domesticated species, we have also selected for females that reach puberty earlier than their wild ancestors.

Having a fertile bitch around the home can lead to many problems in her life, as well as those described earlier that affect us. We are usually most unwilling to have her come home pregnant to produce a litter of bouncy puppies sixty-three days or so after every one of her seasons, that is, twice or three times a year for a breeding life of about ten years. But if she isn't mated and doesn't conceive when her body is ready to because we keep her safe from the attentions of any hopeful males that have beat a path to our door, her hormonal status enters a phase known as metoestrous. This sometimes can cause some very distressing behavioural responses, both for her and for us to watch and experience in our shared den, as we shall see in the next chapter.

DOMINANCE MOUNTING

Dear Mr Neville

Our five-year-old Boxer cross male dog, Fred, has recently taken to mounting our six-year-old son, Tommy. It doesn't occur that often but obviously causes Tommy some distress, but he also laughs quite a lot and calls Fred a 'dirty dawg', though we're sure that he doesn't quite understand what is happening. Fred isn't normally a sexy dog and doesn't seem to be sexually aroused during these episodes which usually last only a few seconds before Tommy effects an escape or Fred simply drops down. The mounting occurs most often when they are playing together with either

Tommy's toys or Fred's chews and toys. Otherwise there are no problems at all between them, in fact Fred seems devoted to Tommy and enjoys playing with him indoors and out without ever a growl or cry heard. Should we be more careful about letting them play together and would castrating Fred help?

Yours sincerely

Desmond Nielsen

Like Bessie, Fred is simply trying to communicate in doggy terms to a junior member of his pack. It's just that the form of communication used is easy to misinterpret from the human point of view. Tommy sees Fred as a 'dirty dawg' but his father, though suspecting sexual intent in Fred, has observed that his dog does not appear to be sexually aroused as he briefly mounts his son. His suspicions are right because Fred is simply trying to reinforce his dominant status over Tommy in his pack. For the most part, Fred is still playing with a 'puppy' that he is playing 'uncle' to. He could be safely expected to adjust his views to perceive Tommy as a higher-ranking member of his pack without any conflict as the boy grows older. Indeed, it is quite likely that relations are at the transition stage where Tommy is about to leapfrog over Fred in the hierarchy. The manifestation of this period of confusion is that Fred appears to 'leapfrog' Tommy in a last and non-aggressive effort to maintain his superiority.

The mounting occurs at times when the two are closely involved with each other in play and is undoubtedly more likely to occur with an element of 'overspill' behaviour when Fred is already getting excited in play. But mounting is also likely to occur when there is a focus for their competition such as the availability of a toy or chew, the possession of which can be a symbol of rank. Such possession and display of symbols is called 'trophying' behaviour and helps dogs to define their relative social standing. The rapid alternation of possession common in most games of 'fetch' or 'tug-o'-war' heightens the demand for those symbols and, as the excitement rises, can cause instability in a fragile hierarchy. In very unstable situations or when a competitive dog's relations with any member of the family, especially children, are ill-defined, such objects can become the focus for aggressive competition and the dog learns quickly to use growls and bites in defence of any status symbols he manages to gain possession of. With Fred, who is less socially conscious and very well adjusted in the human pack, the confusion can be tackled by the dog simply breaking off from the games to mount the child in an effort to reaffirm his right to possess the toys and chews and so maintain his higher status. But Desmond shouldn't worry too much as the transition period should soon pass, and safely, as Tommy is increasingly able to dictate the course of the games, walk away from the mounted dog and tell him off (seen as rejection of the advance in a similar manner as when Bessie was growling at Justin) and retain possession of the symbols at will.

While games may focus the competition between them at present, Tommy will be doing many other things as he grows up that dictate the course of Fred's life, such as walking him on a lead or feeding him, and be backed up by his parents, the ultimate top dogs of the group. Fred will soon come to view Tommy as having the right to take and keep possession of toys and chews at will and soon become as unlikely to attempt to mount him as he would his parents. In just a few weeks or months, such mounting would be a grave social error for Fred to make with a higher-ranking member of his pack and he will increasingly learn to limit the expression of his competitive drives to excitement during the games themselves and look to Tommy to direct the play. 'Control the games to control the dog,' as my Association of Pet Behaviour Counsellors' colleague John Rogerson says, and the more support Tommy gets from his parents at this age, the sooner Fred will accept his succession. Castration certainly wouldn't make any difference to frequency or intensity of this type of mounting behaviour as there is no immediate sexual intent behind it. All that is needed for a while is for Desmond and his wife to manage the level of excitement reached during Tommy's games with Fred, to keep the games short and supervised and to make sure that Tommy is seen by Fred to keep possession of all the toys and chews at the end of the games. This will imply that all such trophies are owned by Tommy and simply brought out for play with Fred at his discretion. More accurately from the dog's point of view of course, the appearance of the toys and chews will be interpreted as Tommy trophying his possessions. It will soon be Tommy that encourages Fred to compete but only ever for the dog to lose the game, so reaffirming Tommy's dominance and ever diminishing Fred's perception of having the right to suppress him by mounting him.

ATTENTION-SEEKING SEX

Dear Mr Neville

Every time I have visitors to my house, my mongrel dog, a male called Archie, becomes a complete sex-pest. He follows my friends around with a disgusting leer on his face and sits deliberately opposite them so that he can flash at them. Given half a chance he will try to mount their legs or, if they kick him off, he'll grab a cushion from one of the armchairs and mount it in front of them. I've tried being patient with him but even telling him off or smacking him only gives a temporary respite before he starts up again. Even an anti-male hormone injection didn't help calm him down very much. What should I try next?

Yours sincerely

Cathy Broome

Archie is a typical attention-demander and when I went to see him and Cathy, he simply wouldn't leave us alone. It turned out that he spent virtually all of the time following Cathy around when she was home and was also allowed to sleep on her bed at night, though he was never sexy with her, only her friends. Obviously I qualified as a friend because after a few minutes of eyeing me up, he duly attempted to make mad passionate love to my left leg. But Archie was not a sexy dog *per se*, which is why the anti-male hormone injection had had such little effect. Archie was simply a dog that was so attached to his owner that he couldn't bear for her attention to be diverted away from him on to anyone else. He was, in human terms, a very jealous little dog but one that in canine terms was only trying to protect the key to his security in his pack of two and ensure that his relationship with Cathy was not diluted in any way. On further investigation I established that Archie had employed a range of attention-getting behaviours with Cathy since he was a young puppy. Whenever visitors arrived he used to whine, pace up and down just out of range of her grab, yap, pick up her handbag, bring in her clothes, throw his toys around and bark at the door and Cathy saw the passing of these reactions as a credit to her patience in dealing with her young dog. She had largely succeeded in removing these behaviours from his repertoire through not responding to them. But all that had happened was that when one ruse hadn't worked the clever Archie simply moved on to the next. Finally he found one that worked every time. All he had to do was turn on the sex to find his dear owner embarrassed into action. As the dog fed once from the table produces a dog that begs at meal times for ever more, one such bout of victory was enough to convince him to demand attention in the lewdest way he could. Obviously it was a lucky break when, in his desperate excitement to keep Cathy's eyes on him, he overspilled into a quick mounting session on the first unsuspecting guest's leg. Cathy's immediate and emphatic reaction in shrieking, grabbing his collar and picking him up to hold him on her lap was all that was needed to convince him to use sexual posturing for ever more whenever he felt that their relationship was under challenge.

Archie tended to use mounting quicker with some visitors than others; mainly men. Perhaps I was one of those men that he regarded as friendly with his owner and thus needed the full works without delay. Others, particularly men or women that Cathy didn't know too well, were flashed at if seated or followed lewdly around if they stood up. Such are the extremes to which a dog may learn to go in the human pack if he feels that he must have his owner's undivided attention. For Archie, treatment was not based on close attention to his sexual status. Castration would have had little more effect than the anti-male hormone. Instead we used periods of time-out as a negative pay-off for his antics. Every time he eyed people up lasciviously or flashed or attempted to mount anything when Cathy had guests, he was coolly removed from their company for about two to three minutes. As he had already learned to keep out of grabbing range, he spent the next couple of weeks following my visit wearing a fairly long trailing lead to facilitate quick interventions. Initially, he continued as he had taught himself to. Like the begging dog who doesn't get a titbit from the table, an occasional failure doesn't extinguish the behaviour if the rewards are

still potentially valuable enough. But after only a week of temporary short banishments as necessary when guests called, the number of attempts to attract Cathy's attention using any sort of behaviour, sexual or otherwise, diminished markedly and the intensity of his efforts dropped. Within a few more days he could be interrupted with a 'no' from Cathy and, by the end of the second week, had become content to lie quietly on the floor near Cathy and her guests and share her. It was certainly preferable to not being in her company at all, it just took a couple of weeks to convince him that pretend sex was not a successful ploy in the pursuance of his aims.

5
Heavy Petting

'A beast that wants discourse of reason'

WILLIAM SHAKESPEARE, *Hamlet*

All the cases of sex or those that looked like sex highlighted in the previous chapter were at least comprehensible from the point of view of the pet trying to fit in and know where and how to stand in its relationship with its human owners. In consultations I find that once the problem is explained, owners often then feel sorry for the confusion that their ownership has caused that particular pet and, despite the serious nature of many of the problems cited, feel strongly motivated to try and readjust their ways and treat those problems to bring about improvements. After all, the dog is never going to be able see life or view his behaviour from the human standpoint, so it's up to the owners to make the effort to communicate at pet level. It gets all the more difficult when our pets demonstrate what looks like sexual behaviour because we can really frustrate or confuse them when we deliberately choose to get more closely involved in their sex lives.

SEX IN DEFENCE OF THE REALM!

Dear Mr Neville

We own a 'pack' of three spayed Yorkshire Terrier bitches and a young similarly sized male mongrel who all get along famously, eating together, sleeping together and playing with their toys... until the doorbell rings. At this signal they all charge to the door, barking like fury to frighten off the visitor. Unfortunately they then fall into total disarray and forget about their territorial defence task altogether. Still barking, the bottom-of-the-pack bitch leaps on the back of the number two in a frantic attempt to mount her, while number two, if she can break free, attempts to do likewise to the top bitch. Sometimes, these altercations lead to fights between Mollie (No. 2) and Mimi (No. 3) but never involving Maggie, the top bitch. The castrated male, Marmaduke, dances around the confusion, trying to mount no one but barking his encouragement and darting in and out to spread the confusion. Do we own a pack of latent lesbian bitches and a male who is too afraid or unsure to attempt to mount any of them, even when sex seems to be the order of the day, or are they all simply getting overexcited when the bell rings? Certainly, once the visitor has been let in, the dogs all calm down and go back to being friendly again. So if their behaviour is sexual in origin, it must be unique in being triggered exclusively by such a Pavlovian stimulus!

Yours sincerely

Miranda and Allan Willis

Some human-monopolised dog packs are, in fact, only stable in the presence of the owners, or are like timebombs on short fuses. Any weakening among the officer owners or higher-ranking dogs up front and the troops may fall into disarray, squabbling among themselves and temporarily all fancying their chances of rising up through the ranks and becoming the breeding animals. This can apply even with sterilised bitches as competition within the group is not simply about sex. Breakdowns in order can cause fighting of a fairly serious nature to occur between members of either sex, though aggression is usually restricted to those of like sex, there usually being little conflict ever between the sexes in dog packs. For other groups of dogs or bitches with hierarchies that are only just stable under normal conditions, and with or without the capping influence of human 'pack leaders' on competitiveness, any rise in background excitability or general arousal can cause a breakdown with fights breaking out when visitors call or the food bowls appear. In the Willis pack, matters are indeed unstable, but not quite so precarious for fights to break out regularly when the excitement level rises. Things may not be so serious because the problem concerns the rank order in a group of bitches rather than between more competitive males, who, in similar circumstances, would almost certainly be guaranteed to start fighting, and seriously, rather than mounting each other to resolve their differences.

The problem in the Willis household is at least consistent. As soon as the doorbell rings, each bitch attempts to seize the opportunity of the confusion of the moment and attempts to mount the next highest ranking female while she is distracted in order to decline her status. Meanwhile, the top bitch is doing her best to lead the pack's defence against the common invader who rang the doorbell. The castrated male, who is not part of the bitches' hierarchy but is in a male one all on his own, without having formed a 'breeding pair' relationship with the top bitch, simply gets excited with all the commotion. He dashes in and barks, perhaps in an attempt to restore order and calm things down, but fails miserably, because none of the bitches perceive him as having any authority and he has no bearing on their immediate status problems.

The mass orgy appearance of the dogs' reactions to the sound of the doorbell bore some resemblance to the decline and fall of the Roman Empire with sex, violence and social disorder rampant at the borders of the territory, in the Willis pack of Yorkies, only the violence and disorder were occurring in reality and the mounting behaviour between the bitches had nothing to do with sex, and certainly not lesbianism! Treatment lay in the ultimate and accepted top-dogs, Miranda and Allan, exerting greater canine style control on all their dogs, but paying special attention to ensure that they reacted with their dogs in strict rank order. Maggie was always to be fed and fussed first and attention for Mollie and Mimi reserved for when she was asleep or elsewhere and always to be applied in rank order.

The problem bitch, as in so many cases involving a troublesome triple of dogs, proved to be the Number 2, Mollie. Mimi was more than happy to stay at the bottom of the heap and take what was going. She had no problem in accepting the new rules from her owners and ceased getting involved with the ructions at the door almost immediately after I had seen this case, preferring instead to bark from wherever she was when the bell rang. Number 1, Maggie, appropriately named after the British Prime Minister of the day, certainly revelled in her reinforced position at the top. But Mollie, freed from the encumbrances of challenge from below, had to be physically restrained for a while during arranged rings at the door as she grudgingly came to accept second place in the canine scheme of things. Once allowed to run free with the others again when the bell rang, she then used to look round to see if her owners were present before attempting her old mounting tricks on Maggie, but would happily accept a loud 'MOLLIE!' yelled from any quarter as a signal to restrict her activities to guarding barks when visitors called. When the dogs were left alone to guard the home, Mollie was put in a room on her own, secure from the others and so unable to take advantage of the temporary loss of the owners' capping influence on her behaviour. Marmaduke, lucky chap, was allowed to carry on as before with no change advised in his relationship with anybody . . . which meant that he could be the one to be spoiled and doted on by Miranda and Allan whenever they felt the need to break the canine rules with one of their doggies and without fear of reversing progress and upsetting stability among the girls.

MY DOG'S IN LOVE WITH A CHAIR!

Dear Mr Neville

There is a very strange male Border Collie called Brock, owned by my wife, who lives in my house. Granted he is very clever and very quick, and has never shown any form of aggression towards either of us or our two children. He occasionally chases the cat, though he knows he shouldn't, but has no other problems in his day-to-day life, until it comes to his sexual preferences. He's never shown any inclination towards sex with any of us, nor with any bitches that he's met on his walks, but whenever he gets excited at home, invariably he first looks confused for a moment, then paces up and down and finally climbs on the soft arm of my armchair and mounts it furiously until he gets pushed off. Is my dog really in love with a chair or is he just plain mad?

Yours, almost as confused as Brock is,

Simon Blair

Brock would have earned himself the honour of portrayal in one of Russell Jones' splendid cartoons that adorn this book, if it weren't for the fact that this was such a sad case. Brock's bizarre relationship with the armchair wasn't caused by some perverted obsession; his behaviour was a rather pitiful, if highly amusing, example of displacement behaviour. Brock had the misfortune, like so many of his breed, to have been taken on by a family that was totally unsuited to keep a Border Collie.

The Blair family lived in a tenth-floor apartment of a high-rise block in the middle of London. Though they started with the best intentions of walking Brock several times a day in the nearby park, the reality was that this poor intelligent sheep herder was lucky to get out for a decent off-lead run more than twice a week and was simply let out onto the balcony to relieve himself for the rest of the time. As a result he was highly reactive within the home and virtually anything that caused him to become excited produced this bizarre pattern of behaviour. Sometimes it would be the sound of the telephone ringing, other times the movement of the cat or strange noise on the television. Mr and Mrs Blair, or their kids arguing or playing, could make Brock mount the armchair or sometimes he just paced round and round, pretending to herd the furniture before finally leaping on to his favourite piece. In time, the desperate Brock, starved of the opportunity to work or exercise his mind and body, came, as did Archie in the previous chapter, to exploit the family's reaction to his strange behaviour by mounting the chair deliberately to get attention. In his mind it was more rewarding to be told off, or even risk a cuff round the ear than be ignored when so little of interest or novelty happened in his life.

The whole performance of this utterly out-of-context instinctive behaviour was borne out of the unresolvable conflicts, stresses and frustrations of his life, and had become a regular and established pattern for poor Brock by the time I called round to see him. For once, I didn't spare the rod with the Blairs and, after explaining why their dog was 'in love with a chair' and that this was not a sexual problem, I made it totally clear that they should find him a new home with an active and understanding owner as soon as possible. I regarded their keeping of him under their existing circumstances as psychologically cruel, and while a lack of understanding of dogs is forgivable, cruelty most definitely is not.

Thankfully, for Brock's sake, the Blair family agreed that they had been rather silly to get him in the first place and, though they loved him, that they could do nothing better to show it than find him a better home. Within a week, they had found a super new home for him in the rolling countryside of Devon in south-west England. Brock lives there to this day, running around and being as active as can be with an owner who just loves to walk him. Never once has he shown any inclination to mount a chair or anything else, except the bitch Border Collie that was brought to him for mating about a year after he arrived.

Not being a chair-obsessed pervert after all, Brock got it all right first time and fathered a super litter of six active little Border Collie bundles. I'm glad to report that they all went to working homes, where most Border Collies find most happiness, even if very few of those that are kept as non-working and rather confined pets show such bizarre displacement behaviour as Brock.

DIM THE LIGHTS, PLAY SOFT MUSIC, LIGHT THE CANDLES . . . AND GET THE MOUNTING BOX OUT!

In amongst the many triggers for Brock's fascination with the armchair were several elements of learned response. Given certain influences, such as the telephone ringing, Brock was guaranteed to mount the chair. While this was clearly originally an attention-getting display, it soon became as conditioned a response as Pavlov's dogs salivating to the sound of a bell.

This very type of conditioning is used by many human suitors who lay on a romantic environment over dinner to relax the person of their desires and put him or her 'in the mood'. Breeders of dogs often do similarly as was nicely demonstrated by a Mastiff breeder I once knew. When her stud male was required to perform with the latest big bitch, all his owner had to do was bring out his mounting box. Originally, this was provided to help him, as a huge, heavy dog, to get up onto the bitch and keep in balanced position while he did the necessary, but after a few matings, he associated the very sight of the box with the prospect of mating and was panting and raring to go whenever he saw it, irrespective of whether a bitch was waiting or not.

In technical learning terms, this is a prime case of classical conditioning and particularly interesting because it could be applied in the primeval context of sexual responses, despite their deep-rooted and instinctive nature. Sometimes, dogs manage to condition themselves to making sexual responses to unusual cues in the absence of any other suitable outlet for their passions. For example, if a dog consistently and exclusively mounts a particular teddy bear or pink elephant, the production of that toy in almost any context or place is very likely to elicit a sexual response. But then, anyone who has ever prepared a sensual meal and put Ravel's *Bolero* on under candlelight with a new girlfriend or boyfriend has usually been banking on exactly the same thing. It just requires a slightly more complicated box as far as we people are concerned!

Mounting boxes aside, we've already seen how complicated the situation can be regarding the prospect of sex for a dog in the human pack. Not only are there restricted opportunities for the adolescent dog to experiment on to develop in this area which compound the natural confusions of this time of life, but the social rules that govern pack life in general are not always exactly what even the adult pet dog has been programmed to expect or have the ability to react to.

It all comes down to the fact that though man and dog are similar, they are obviously not the same. Their communication patterns facilitate a good degree of mutual understanding, but when the more instinctive drives that dictate a dog's sexual attitudes are motivating his or her behaviour, we can find the greatest difficulties in shaping that behaviour to our demands. A good example of this was the understandable but nonetheless intolerable behaviour of dogs such as Merlin as we saw in the previous chapter. And then, there is Helga . . .

NO SEX PLEASE, I'M HUMANISED

Dear Mr Neville

Every time our Dachshund bitch, Helga, comes into season she is as good as gold. There's no fuss, very little mess and we simply keep her away from the boys by exercising her in the garden for a few days. But as soon as the critical time has passed, we know that she and we will usually be in for a rather difficult time. Helga always has a phantom pregnancy about ten weeks after her season, during which she not only produces milk for her non-existent puppies but also becomes rather aggressive in defence of the substitute litter of toys and cushions that she gathers under our sideboard. If we approach her nest at this time, she can turn very nasty, though if we take the time to approach softly and reassure her that we intend no harm, she will usually calm down. If we take her 'puppies' away when she is outdoors, she simply gathers another litter. Our vet has advised us to think carefully about whether we intend to let Helga have a real litter and to have her spayed if we decide not to, but we really can't make up our minds. Can you help us?

Yours sincerely

Clare and Gavin White

This is a sad case of what can and does happen to many fertile bitches in the human pack which are prevented from having sex at the appropriate time and thus denied the opportunity to reproduce because of the plans or demands of their owners. The bitch simply proceeds with her normal sexual cycle, but although prevented from being mated during oestrus, nonetheless enters a period of rather similar hormonal activity as if she was pregnant. This is due to a fall in production of progesterone and accompanying rise in oestrogen after oestrus which is similar to the changes that would have occurred at the time of the birth of her puppies had she been mated. This period of metoestrus can last up to ninety days and the incidence of false or phantom pregnancies is very common, though not usually with such dramatic effects as the Whites encountered with Helga.

The main symptoms, which can include weight gain, increased appetite, abdominal enlargement and even mock contractions, appear at eight to twelve weeks after the bitch would have been mated and would have started to produce milk. Lactation and nest-building are perhaps the most frequently encountered symptoms in pet bitches and these can also occur commonly in wild dog or wolf packs. There it is very useful for a bitch to have a false pregnancy because it enables her to share in the nursing of any litter born at the same time or already being suckled by the breeding bitch in the pack and thus helps ensure their survival and maintain the strength of the pack as a whole. This is not simply a great act of kindness as, being related to the top breeding bitch, she will be helping to ensure the successful perpetuation of many of her own genes. Although the 'auntie' nursing bitch has not been mated, perhaps because she lacks the necessary social standing or she failed to give off the appropriate pheromone attractants to interest a mate, the changes she undergoes nonetheless contribute to the success of the group.

But what of poor Helga, who has no real puppies to assist with in the human pack? The drives are simply so strong that she adopts any likely suitably-sized objects around the home, usually her own toys or clothes and furnishings bearing a concentration of the owners' scent, and nurses and protects them until her hormone levels die away or her milk dries up. Shoes are common substitute puppies and, more sadly in human terms, little girls' dolls can also be found stashed in warm corners by the would-be auntie or mother. In many cases, because the milk is not actually being sucked away, painful mammary infections can set in or, like Helga, her behaviour becomes so unpleasant that the poor dog then requires treatment by the vet with a hormone injection or tablets to bring her artificially out of this hormonal state, and back into her normal sexual cycle. It's all down to lack of sex, either direct or indirect in the dog's human pack, and having occurred once in any bitch, is likely to occur after every season she has.

Clearly we should now question the justification of keeping bitches such as Helga in a fertile condition if they are to be denied the opportunity to breed on one hand but expected to go through pain and confusion at least twice per year because of the effects of their reproductive hormones on their behaviour. The veterinary treatment to relieve the symptoms of phantom pregnancies may well be simple, virtually risk-free and usually totally and quickly effective, but is this type of management really to be condoned? It is surely a rather unpleasant price for any pet to have to pay for a life in the human pack when there is a permanent answer available if only the Whites would make the simple decision not to have puppies from Helga and have her surgically spayed.

Finally we have come to consider sterilising at least some of our bitches for their own well-being and to save them from the natural effects of their own normal reproductive cycles. One could argue that this is an even more unpleasant price to pay for a life in the human den than a hormone jab or tablets in the control of false pregnancies, but at least spaying is preventative rather than curative after the discomfort and confusion of the condition has begun. And what choice do owners like the Whites really have when their normally sexually

functioning bitch is denied the opportunity to mate or raise a litter of her own and further denied the type of social environment where she could even play nursemaid to the breeding pair's offspring? The nursemaid role couldn't happen in the human pack because the breeding pair are of a different species, one that feeds its children with milk from a plastic bottle if and when the parents decide that it's not convenient to feed the real stuff — that and our natural resistance to letting the dog feed the baby!

Of course, most owners of bitches like Helga eventually make the decision not to breed from their pet and have her sterilised to save her from going through her sexual cycle and enduring its associated hormone changes, and rightly so. Many other owners and breeders have their vet suppress the sexual cycles of their bitches with the same hormone injection or tablets so that they do not come on heat at all when due and thus also do not suffer the aftermath of false pregnancies. This option can be useful to give breeding bitches a rest or keep them out of season for important engagements at dog shows or to enable the owners to go on holiday without causing widespread disruption among the boy dogs at the boarding kennel (most kennels won't accept bitches in season for this very reason). But there is no doubt that the kindest thing to do for all non-breeding bitches is to sterilise them. And as I also believe that dog-breeding should be solely in the hands of regulated registered specialists, any bitch kept purely as a pet really should be spayed as soon as the vet advises it is safe to do so. Forget all the nonsense about a bitch needing to have a litter to be fulfilled or to develop her character . . . there's no evidence whatsoever that this is the case. If all pet bitches are spayed, then neither they nor their owners have to suffer from the physical or behavioural effects of her being on heat discussed in Chapter 2, nor the common aftermath of phantom pregnancies that poor Helga went through.

TIPPING IS DISCRETIONARY!

Dear Mr Neville

I would like to breed from my Birman queen, Sophie, but would like her to grow up a little and have two or three seasons before doing so. I know that my vet can give her something to stop her from calling but I've also heard that I can stop her once she's started by physical means that mimic mating. Is this as unpleasant as it sounds and will she suffer at all, assuming that it is done correctly?

Yours sincerely

Cynthia Williams

In contrast with many of their dog-owning counterparts, cat owners are already used to having their pets sterilised at about six months of age. This is because the behavioural consequences of not doing so are widely known and generally accepted as being too inconvenient for the pet owner to want to risk suffering from. Breeding of pedigree strains is largely in the hands of specialist breeders or very keen amateurs who know what to expect and how to manage it, though alas, there are still far too many surplus-to-requirements 'surprise' litters of moggie kittens born every year to unsuspecting, misguided or uncaring owners of entire queens. The harsh reality of false pregnancies often finally forces the decision to spay a bitch by dog owners who are prepared to put up with the actual period of heat, but with cats, other options are available. Their calling behaviour during their heat can be artificially brought to a close by a vet or other expert armed with a cotton bud because, as we saw in Chapter 2, cats are post-coital ovulators. The cotton bud is inserted into the vagina very carefully to irritate the walls in the same way as the tom's barbed penis and so stimulate ovulation and bring the oestrous period to a close. It's a potentially very risky business, not least because the queen may turn round and take a swipe at you as you remove the cotton bud in the same way as she would at a withdrawing tom, but most risk, of course, is borne by the poor cat and so this really is a procedure only for experts. It may also only bring temporary relief to the battered eardrums of the owners as the cat may come on call again only a day or so later.

But, in any case, are such indelicate physical intrusions into the sexual life and anatomy of the female cats that we choose to keep in breeding condition really any more justified than our hormonal management of bitches like Helga? Our pets are, after all, simply passing through their sexual cycles in our homes as their genes have always dictated since long before we adopted them as companion animals. As with bitches, the sexual cycle of female cats can also be suppressed with artificial hormone preparations available from the vet, but surely every non-breeding female cat should be spared this type of treatment in the name of breeding control of our pet cats?

The question is whether we, as the ultimate controllers of our pets' behaviour and lifestyle, can accept their sexual responses as part of the deal. For many pet owners, controlling the sex life of their pets is little or poorly understood and a nuisance and, when evident, is often something unexpected that they would rather wasn't there. And, in 'stiff-upper-lip' Britain at least, as we would often prefer not to acknowledge the strong sexual drives that develop in our children as they grow up, facing reality with our pets is often even less likely. The exhibition of sexual behaviour, real and normal, displaced or aberrant, comes as a rude awakening that our pets, like our children, do grow up and become sexually functioning adults like us. The onset of physical maturity and sexual awareness signals the end of 'baby-days' in our children and that parental close protection and nurturing must now be relaxed and steadily replaced with a period of careful guidance as our kids become teenagers and then grown up. But while we can simply enjoying playing the nurturing role for our pets while we are also raising our children, we can continue expressing such caring emotions to our pets long after our kids have fled the nest. And as neoteny, the maintenance of infantile characteristics, in cats and dogs especially is something that we have deliberately selected for and bred into them, it suits us fine that part of our relationship enables us to play a parental role with our pets throughout their lives. But the harmony of that thoroughly enjoyable relationship is often shattered with the appearance of sexual behaviour in our pets which comes as a rude reminder not only that they too become adult members of their species, but that they are still members of a different species to us, and that they are not real members of our family, no matter how humanised they have become. Sex is just one example of how they follow many natural instincts, drives and motivations which we are often unable to influence.

Fortunately, but perhaps rather too easily, everything in 'that department' can usually be made easy for us with a simple trip to the veterinarian. He or she can satisfy our desire to keep problem-free, stylised pets that are humanised and that will blend in well with our family and obey our social rules, like the sterilised bitch, or at least not upset or challenge them, like the neutered tom. In our modern hectic lifestyles it increasingly implies that we must control the sexual side of our pets' natures by standard physical or medical means if they are to fit comfortably into our schemes of life, yet we increasingly fail to realise that their innate drives for survival and the sexual or other expression of those drives will persist, irrespective of our expectations. Perhaps we would prefer not even to think about it in order to preserve the cosiness of our relationship in many or most cases.

But then we too can be confused about our relationship with our pets. On the one hand we welcome our pets into our homes as members of the family and happily confess to treating them 'like children' or 'spoiling' them and generally being very anthropomorphic about them. We spend billions of dollars, pounds, francs, etc, every year ensuring their well-being in our families while we do what would be unthinkable for a human family member by either totally restricting or totally controlling their sexual and reproductive behaviour. It's no wonder that many people find it difficult to have their pets sterilised when they have such close relationships with them. To them it is indeed like having your son or daughter sterilised. And it's no wonder that some owners need the really unbearable or pitiful reality of a queen calling all night, a dog sexually mounting their children or a bitch attempting to nurse their slippers before they finally get their relationship with their pet back into perspective. Only then may they realise that they have little choice in the matter if they are to keep their pet as part of the family in the way that they want to. They have to come to terms with the fact that a dog is a dog and a cat is a cat and not a furry human and accept that their pets can only fill the role as 'pets for man' if they are asexual. The only way to justify such interference with their natural drives is to view them accurately, because when it comes to sex, if we view them as almost human, we would be ethically unable to control their reproductive cycles and associated behaviour. This problem is well illustrated by our attitude towards our pets when they breed or try to breed with their own close relatives.

INCEST

'One should try everything once, except incest and folk-dancing' ARNOLD BAX

Dear Mr Neville

I have just returned from the vet with my eight-month-old Persian cat, Fluff, having been told that she is pregnant. I am distraught, because I made absolutely sure to keep her indoors when she was calling and chased away all the feral toms who appeared in my garden. She spent the whole time with her brother, who isn't yet castrated and so only he can have done the deed. Surely he wouldn't have mated with his own sister. Has he no shame? Now I'll have to have the kittens aborted and him castrated without delay.

Yours sincerely

Belinda Lewis

Well, if as we discussed earlier, animals don't have a moral sense, they're hardly likely to develop social taboos about incest. Those taboos are, of course, designed to prevent breeding between close relatives to avoid the perpetuation of any heritable defects and, in turn, to ensure that the stability of the bond between the parents and the social group is maintained. Obviously this is less important with cats than with wolves, wild dogs or with man, as the tom cat father plays no essential role in the upbringing of his kittens, though pet dogs, too, mate promiscuously and simply in response to the appropriate chemical cues. Belinda's young tom certainly would not stop to think, 'I shouldn't mate with my sister,' any more than he would in the wild if he happened to encounter her. He fails to recognise her as a relative and does what comes naturally even in the human den because he is in contact with her at the appropriate biological time. In the wild or feral cat, genes are kept spread and the likelihood of inbreeding reduced by the dispersal of kittens, toms especially, away from the maternal nest as they enter adolescence. With wild dogs and wolves, the offspring remain in the pack, but the internal social disciplines and perhaps detachment of male gangs from the pack that we have discussed earlier ensure that close inbreeding remains unlikely. However, the top breeding pair will invariably be related to some extent and perpetuate the success of the majority of the pack's common genes without the risks of direct relatives, for example brother and sister, father and daughter, mating, or at least not for too many succeeding generations. It's a fine balance, of course, but it seems to work. In the human den, however, there are no such long-term constraints and any dog will mate with any bitch and any tom with any queen with no social holds or thoughts of human-style morals. Your fault, Belinda. Don't be disgusted, just try to understand your pets better and forget about applying human morals to their behaviour!

Most owners now regard sterilisation as a normal aspect of pet keeping for the young animal and then go on afterwards to anthropomorphise their pet once there is no longer any risk of any unwanted genuine sexual behaviour and conflicts over their own taboos to spoil things. But there are a few owners who fail to come to terms with the necessary adjustment in attitude between regarding their pet as a human family member and an instinctive creature. This can lead to the most bizarre confusions as owners struggle to come to terms with their pet's sexuality by means other than sterilisation or chemical control. Mr Arthur in the introduction 'Foreplay' tried his best to accommodate the sexual side of Robbie, his Jack Russell, by allowing himself to be mounted rather than have his close family member and companion castrated. But, believe it or not, I have seen people driven to even greater confusion regarding what to do with their pet's sexuality.

A DOG IN THE HAND . . . YUK!

Dear Mr Neville

My wife and I own a tough West Highland White Terrier called Snowy. We have many problems with him, not least being the fact that he can sometimes be very aggressive towards us both and towards other male dogs. He is usually friendly with bitches and perhaps more tolerant of my wife giving him commands and grooming him than he is of me. Ever since he was about ten months old he has always been a sexy little so-and-so, mounting cushions, his bed blankets and even our legs on a fairly regular basis. I felt rather sorry for Snowy, after all he has no other dogs for company and we simply don't have the space to take on any more. My wife and I have discussed this at length and decided that the kindest thing to do was to relieve his sexual frustration manually whenever he became sexually aroused rather than tell him off, and this we have been doing for about a year. He has come to expect such relief and sometimes he wants it every evening, though he may go several days without demanding. Our efforts seem to have helped reduce his sexual frustration and the need to masturbate with his bedding, though he does seem to be a little more aggressive with me these days. Am I making a rod for my own back with regard to Snowy's aggression by trying to help relieve him sexually in this way?

Yours sincerely

Mr and Mrs X (for absolute anonymity!)

I could hardly believe this as I listened to it. Mr and Mrs X sat opposite me with the clearly rather dominant Snowy perched on Mr X's lap and, in quite normal tones, described in effect, that they loved their dog so much that they felt it perfectly normal to cater for him in this way. There were a billion problems in their relationship with Snowy, most of them related to the fact that he was one of those male dogs simply born to be a pack leader and a breeder. He had been lucky enough to find a human pack that was prepared to let him, even though it meant that he bit them both on a fairly regular basis, totally dictated their lifestyle and forced them into behaving so very strangely to accommodate his character and try to reduce the need for him to be frustrated and nasty.

I had some sympathy with their position. They were middle-aged and child-less and clearly desperately wanted something around the home to nurture and love. They had deliberately picked a type of dog that is normally fun, extrovert and small enough to be a lap dog to fuss. It was hardly Mr and Mrs X's fault that they picked one really unpleasant and nastily dominant little example and I certainly couldn't blame them for trying to ameliorate his aggression in any way possible. They didn't and couldn't hurt him, nor even bring themselves to tell him off when he was horrid, and rejecting him was utterly out of the question. And as for considerations of castration . . . well, I think their vet had decided not to get involved in the emotional minefield and simply said, 'Well, I'm not sure I can help . . . but I know a man who can!'

And there they were in front of me, a pair of otherwise normal, educated human beings dragged into such a pitiful state because of the way that they viewed their dog. Being only human myself, I just had to leave the room for a few minutes after hearing the Xs' tale before I tackled the thorny subject of treatment. My good friend, the equally anonymous vet who kindly rented me the facilities I was consulting in, had been operating on a cat in the next room and, with his nurse, had overheard through the thin walls. He wasn't intending to eavesdrop and, being the epitome of professionalism, never normally ventured any comment about my cases unless I asked him. But, like anyone else in such close proximity to such an incredible tale, he just couldn't help himself. As I left the room, I caught sight of him leaning against the wall, operating gown askew and one hand cupped over his mouth, while the other wiped away the tears with a clean surgical swab. His nurse, blushing, was already beyond speech.

Mr Vet, an Irishman through and through, had lapsed into the broadest brogue in his emotional collapse. 'I used to tink I had it tuff out here cutt'n up people's loved ones,' he gasped, 'and help'n 'em come to terms wid it all when de beast's had enuff, but you've got yer work cut out in there all right, me lad.' He slid slowly down the wall until he sat with his legs stuck out towards the middle of the surgery, desperately fighting for breath and letting the tears roll down his cheeks. His nurse ran out into the garden in search of fresh air and the cat on the table sighed. They'd just managed to get through repairing the cut to its leg in time before decorum vanished and now it was starting to stir as it came out of the light anaesthetic. I left 'yer man' in a heap and went and made some coffee for myself and my clients. As I passed him on the way back, he was still in the same position, utterly helpless, but managed to wheeze, 'Yer'll earn yer money all right wit dat hoolly of a dog, but it's just lead-deficient, lad. Shall I call me mate at the psychiatric school for de owners?' And then he started wheezing again.

For those interested, my consultation with Mr and Mrs X proceeded as normal and after explaining at length about the nature of dogs and their relationships, how dominance and sex could be tied up and that confusion was the predominating state of mind for Snowy, they agreed that they would have to restructure their relations with him. They would try their best to treat him as a low-ranking dog in their family rather than as a child, though, of course if parents did what they did to their dog, they would find themselves in serious trouble. (The whole treatment for this type of dog is outlined in my earlier book, *Do Dogs Need Shrinks?*.)

Because much of Snowy's dominant behaviour and sexual activity was clearly inspired by the hormone levels typical of such canine characters, we also agreed that if not for the sake of human decency, then for the sake of Snowy's state of mind, he should be castrated without delay. Irrespective of the unwanted sexual activity, it's a must for this type of serious dominance problem and one I never have any hesitation in recommending for the dominant dog in the human pack. On its own, research has shown that castration would only have about a fifty-fifty chance of curing Snowy's behaviour, but combined with relationship restructuring, the chances would be far higher, and especially because Snowy was still only two years of age. The chances of curing such behaviour through any form of treatment certainly tail off after the dog is socially as well as sexually mature and are almost negligible with, say, a five-year-old dog, whose patterns of behaviour will have become well-ingrained and long ago will have ceased to be exclusively hormone inspired. Despite the learned explanations, Mr and Mrs X were, as I expected, crestfallen at the prospect of castration for their little darling but I explained, as carefully as I could, that the paths that he would make for himself in a dog pack simply were not available to him in a human pack, no matter how nice and accommodating they were to him in human terms. It all simply reinforced his nasty side and put them at risk. They had a special type of dog, one that needed treating as a dog more than any other kind and relieving his sexual frustrations would only make it worse for them all. I'm glad to say that they followed the suggestions to the letter and that it all worked. Mr and Mrs X now own a tough but happier dog and, having ceased to cater long ago to their dog's sexual appetite, can hold their heads up in polite company. But my lasting memory of this case will be the sight of Mr Vet in the corner of my eye, but hidden behind a partition wall from Mr and Mrs X as I showed them out, grasping his knee with both hands like Basil Fawlty in an effort to keep his emotions under control. The cat, somewhat surprisingly under the circumstances, made a perfect and uneventful recovery!

But, if this case has reached hitherto unplumbed depths in this book written towards the end of the liberal twentieth century, the following chapters will take you still further down.

6
Man Plays God

'The best method of birth control is to make your husband sleep on the roof' MARGARET STAFFORD

Moving quickly back to the firmer footing of more scientific discussion, the one overriding purpose of life is survival of our genes through individuals. But it is the adaptation of individuals to their environment that facilitates that genetic success through their changing structure, physiology and behaviour. Every organism must be adapted to its environment otherwise it would die. So if the environment changes it must adapt to cope and reproduce itself in a slightly different form to avoid, for example, the fate of the dinosaurs in the face of rising temperature and carbon dioxide levels, or the similar and quicker end met by the Dodo when it failed to adapt to avoid man, the new two-legged predator arriving in Mauritius. All successful adaptations in a creature's ability to defend itself against attack by other animals and search out food and appropriate shelter are designed to ensure that it can continue to reproduce its genetic material for ever, yet the very process of domestication of our current popular mammalian pets, the cat and dog, reduces and controls their innate capability for survival. Instead of being shaped by their adaptability to their natural environment, they are now shaped by us according to our demands and this has, of course, lead to many changes in their original physical and physiological design.

We are, in effect, playing God with the breeding of our domestic species. It's a role with a clear aim of producing more food from those animals domesticated for the purpose such as cattle or chickens, but perhaps with less justifiable aims in our pets which are kept solely as our companions. For dogs, cats, rabbits and the like, our aim is to make them better able to share our company in a friendly manner for the sake of our own safety, make them more directable at certain tasks or controllable in our den or in the environments that we make for them, and to alter their physical appearance in ways that appeal to us. This has even led us to produce breeds of dog that need help to be able to mate, for example, some of the larger breeds such as Mastiffs may require the breeder to lift the male onto the back of the female because, despite being aflame with the most ardent of desires, he is not strong enough to be able to lift his own bulk into the appropriate position. Once up, he may also need help with inserting his penis into the right place, but then stallions and bulls have been helped along with that most vital of aims for almost as long as horses and cattle have been domesticated by us.

Of perhaps even greater concern to the welfare of the bitch of certain breeds of dog is the fact they now produce such big litters or pups which are so large that natural birth has become very risky. For example, the bitch of a breed of dog that I have loved and kept, the Large Munsterlander, often requires a caesarean section for the puppies to be born safely and to reduce the risk of killing their mother in the process. Safer it may be, but is this what we have come to in our efforts to produce dogs of a size, shape, hair colour and length to suit us? For many breeds of dog, their whole reproductive opportunity and 'success' is now entirely in the hands of man, or rather, a specific type of person who gets involved with breeding that particular type. That involvement may demand assistance at mating, arranging for caesarean sections, bottle feeding and weaning of puppies and monitoring genetic influences with regard to heritable disease or undesirable behaviour traits. In so doing they are virtually taking on the whole role of Mother Nature, but, of course, can't hope to do it nearly as well as when her principle of survival of the fittest is largely replaced by the grossly less divine principles of survival of the prettiest or survival of the best workers that man applies.

Alas, in amongst the unnatural genetic turmoil that we often create in our pets, the strongest, deepest instinctive drive to reproduce persists, however we manage to shape the beast or change certain areas of his behaviour. As this book has shown, it is this very urge that can lead to so many of the difficulties that we have with our pets, even though some of them have been humans' companions for thousands of years. If our designs and abilities to influence the fundamental urge can't proceed fast enough at the species level, or some of our pets continue to show unbearable departures from the comfortable average then we often resort to making changes at the individual level. All through our look at the sexual nature of the pet so far, we have seen that an owner's first reaction, and usually the first advice received from their veterinary surgeon in the face of unwanted sexual behaviour in their pet, is to sterilise it. In fact, surgical sterilisation has become an almost standard procedure for all cats and dogs, if not for rabbits, in most of the western world.

True, the main rationale behind this is that we have always produced, or allowed to be produced, far too many cats and dogs for the number of available homes and this overpopulation alone is the cause of much unnecessary suffering. Euthanasia carried out by us of those cats and dogs excess to our requirements is one of the leading causes of mortality in the two species. I, like anyone concerned about animal welfare and the sanctity of life, am appalled by the numbers of healthy cats and dogs destroyed every year by animal welfare and rescue societies, municipal stray cat and dog pounds and veterinary surgeons for the sole reason that, despite having been made by humans for the purpose, no human being can be found to make them into pets. And so, naturally, I am firmly of the opinion that all pets not required for carefully controlled (and preferably licensed, though this is rarely the case) breeding programmes should be sterilised in order to reduce the numbers born 'accidentally' simply to be destroyed later. Surgical castration and spaying not only ensures that we don't have to worry about unwanted litters, removal of the sexual hormones also curbs many of the excesses of male and female behaviour that, however natural, we find undesirable in the pets that we keep in the human pack. There's no doubt that removing behaviour inspired by sex hormones generally makes them more consistent and easier to manage, especially for those (most of us) who want to have animals around them but cannot or will not find the time to accommodate even the normal sexual nature of their pets, let alone those who suffer with genuinely difficult pet sex problems.

However, in the United Kingdom at least, while pet cats of both sexes do tend to take an early trip to the vet for some permanent surgery, most male dogs and many bitches are maintained in a fertile state. For some owners, there is a genuine fear of the risk to their pet's life that the anaesthetic and surgery may present, despite the fact that veterinary medicine is so advanced and accidents are so rare as to make the car journey to the veterinarian probably more risky than the surgery itself. But the fear is understandable, given the close present-day nature of most owners' relationships with their pets, a closeness that leads to the type of extreme confusions in some of the cases I have cited when owners try to deal with some of the sexual problems presented by their pets. Unlike humans, our cats, dogs, rabbits and other pets do not seem to have psychological problems in coming to terms with being castrated or spayed, nor with receiving injections or tablets designed to curb their libido or reproductive cycles. We, on the other hand, can't help but anthropomorphise about them and worry that, by having them sterilised, we will destroy some enjoyable aspect of their lives and often question our own moral right to interfere in such an expedient way.

For other owners, the cost of the surgery can sometimes be prohibitive, despite the relatively low cost of veterinary treatment in the United Kingdom compared with the USA and much of the rest of Northern Europe, and the availability of many cut-price neutering schemes offered by animal welfare societies. In southern Europe there is often a cultural resistance to having male animals neutered, a problem that I encountered time and time again when running an animal shelter in Greece. So many owners just wouldn't even consider having their tom cat or male dog castrated because of the macho connotations and 'denial' of the right to be a fully functioning male with the necessary equipment intact. And while a few are less concerned about removing the breeding capabilities of their queens or their bitches, the general direction of improvement at least in Greece was usually to control pets' sexual cycles chemically rather than through irreversible surgery, though in true Greek fashion, many would forget from time to time and so still contribute to the problem of overpopulation.

The cultural aspects of western-style pet-keeping have clearly been embraced in many Mediterranean regions, both in the Latin countries to the north and the

Arab lands to the south. The standard of individual care of those pets is not as bad as we might assume in many cases and attitudes are improving all the time, with the sole exception of control of numbers. The reluctance to sterilise is born out of the underlying religious belief that fertility is given to all animals by God and no man should take it away. It is reinforced by the macho opinions rife in male-dominated human societies. The net result is millions of unwanted puppies and kittens being born every year and either being killed at birth, turfed out onto the street as soon as they are weaned or taken to beleaguered animal welfare organisations that are forced simply to become euthanasia camps for all those excess dogs and cats, puppies and kittens. Suggesting birth control to help prevent the stray problem is tough enough in such countries, especially as many are Catholic and ideologically opposed to birth control for people, but suggesting neutering in the treatment of behaviour problems in cats and dogs is almost unthinkable. And if the western humanisation of cats and dogs leads to confusions in the nature of the relationship when it comes to the sexual behaviour of pets, compound it with religious beliefs and a macho society and the chances for sanity look slim indeed once the Mediterranean cat or dog is allowed right in to share the human den from his more traditional place outdoors in the yard.

But it's not only a Mediterranean attitude that can cause problems for our pet species. In Sweden it is not permitted legally for owners to have their bitch spayed or their male dog castrated without a good medical reason. Quite apart from any lost benefits in respect of problem behaviour management, the implications on the population size of dogs, or, more accurately, unwanted dogs, are obviously severe. It's a classic case of according human emotions to pets on a national scale that it is totally out of keeping with the specific needs and demands of those pets within the human den. One of the direct repercussions of the law is that, since it was passed far more bitches have since been presented to vets in need of an emergency spay because of womb infections that would naturally not have occurred if their womb had been removed in the first place. The risk of death caused by such delay in surgery is far, far greater than that of a standard spay, carried out on a fit pet bitch to sterilise her when she is old enough, as practised throughout the rest of the western pet-keeping world.

VASECTOMIES FOR PETS?

Dear Mr Neville

I am fully aware that as I do not wish to breed from Jones, my tom cat, I should make sure that he cannot father lots of unwanted kittens around the place. However, I am very reluctant to have him castrated as I feel he has a right to enjoy life as a male. I wondered whether it is possible for him to have a vasectomy instead, so that he can rush around with any nice female cats he meets but only fire blanks when he has sex. Are there any drawbacks on the behavioural front to this?

Yours sincerely

Bill King

Bill is clearly well aware of his responsibilities in not having lots of little Joneses running around the world, but through putting himself in his cat's place is worried that Jones will not lead a 'normal' sex life. But while vasectomies are certainly possible for cats and dogs and will indeed render male animals infertile, the operation doesn't remove the testicles, the source of male hormone production. So the dog or tom continues to behave as a normal, fully-functioning male animal. Unless the dog is being specifically aggressive to other males or showing definite sexual problems related to his hormonal status, then vasectomy can be a rather sweet way of accommodating the human view of sexuality and the need to limit populations of dogs. For tom cats, however, testosterone-related behaviour may be the undoing of the very human/pet relationship.

Though infertile, Jones would continue to be motivated to roam perhaps far from home in search of mates, to fight other males including those which are neutered but especially other entire or vasectomised toms, will still spray very pungent urine around his territory, and quite likely indoors. But worse, in the high-density cat populations of suburbia, Jones is likely to suffer more and more injury and resultant infection from his altercations with other cats as he gets older and less able to take on the local tough guys. So, while he may be getting plenty of sex with the local unspayed alley girls, the price of being effectively a full tom in a human environment will be high on him and perhaps not worth it from the point of view of the hygiene of Bill's home and the vet bills he'll bring him in return. In fact, the only benefit would probably be a slight reduction in the number of litters produced by the feral queens that Jones mates with. After all, they will ovulate after he has mated with them but unless other fertile toms follow him, there will be no sperm deposited to enable conception and that season in the queens will not produce kittens. Indeed, rather than use the cotton bud to cause queens to ovulate mentioned earlier, some cat breeders keep a vasectomised tom for this very purpose and to bring their queens off call when they don't want them to have a litter that particular season.

REINCARNATION VS CASTRATION

Speaking, as we were, of religious views regarding the neutering of pets, my dear friend and fellow behaviourist Roger Abrantes from Denmark tells the hilarious tale of a Buddhist client who was referred to him with an aggressive dog to treat. Roger felt that castration was indicated for the dog's problem but his client politely informed him that he believed his Pekingese was the reincarnation of his father and thus such measures were totally out of the question! Poor Roger had to think again as indeed do all we pet shrinks when faced with absolute rejection of castration by owners who regard their pet very much as a member of the human family and thus to be accorded human rights, including the right to retain their masculinity.

There are a great many households locked in disagreement over this castration issue, and a fair few are referred by vets to behaviourists for more in-depth discussions about the problem than they have time to offer in veterinary practice. Often the wife is quite relaxed

about having the dog castrated, whether for birth control, or problem prevention in a young dog as a standard procedure, or as a later measure to help treat an unexpected behavioural problem. But the husband, fuelled by feelings of sympathy and empathy and, perhaps, the feeling that he could be next, digs his heels in to fight to keep the dog's testicles where they are: on the dog. Occasionally it's the other way around with the lady of the house defending those two bits but, in my experience, men are at best unconcerned about castration, and at worst, blindingly and defensively obsessed!

KEEPING UP APPEARANCES

Dear Mr Neville

I realise that much of the aggression that my Rottweiler, Kurt, shows towards me and other male dogs is due to his hormones and, after much soul-searching following our discussion, have decided to take your advice and arrange to have him castrated. My problem is that as Kurt is short-haired and has a docked tail, everyone will be able to see that he is not a male anymore afterwards. I think I will look rather silly walking along the street with a large powerful dog that has been castrated, so I was wondering whether it is possible for Kurt to be fitted with artificial implants at the same time as his real testicles are removed that will keep up his male appearance. How much is this likely to cost, assuming it is possible?

Yours sincerely

Brian Smith

There has been a growth in popularity of keeping large short-haired and traditionally docked breeds like Dobermanns and Rottweilers in recent times, and sadly all too often by people who see their dog as a reflection, extension or substitute for their own character or image. In many cases castration is recommended by vets or behaviourists to assist owners of dogs of assertive and confident large breeds such as Rottweilers, and they encounter not a little degree of resistance to the idea. After all, if you're daft or feeble enough to keep a big tough dog simply to make yourself look more important, then the dog's testicles are bound to be vital parts of your macho outlook on life. The prospect of castrating the dog is that much more painful for you than for the average dog owner, or even the average Rottweiler or Dobermann owner. Dominant individuals of breeds like the Rotty, which has deliberately been selected to be assertive in any case, are quite likely to be recommended for castration more quickly and more frequently than those of less self-confident breeds (though only once per dog, of course!), an interesting paradox considering that images of masculinity feature so high in the breed's popularity.

For Brian Smith, the sensible suggestion of castrating his dog could be made acceptable with no loss to his dignity if Kurt could have prosthetic silicone testicles instead so that no one would know and Brian's macho reputation, as if anyone cared, could remain uncastrated. As it turned out, such replacement was perfectly possible and artificial testicles could indeed be ordered from the catalogue of human prosthetic devices manufactured for use in human medicine and, being about the same size in man and Rottweiler, could be implanted by the vet to create the desired effect. The only stumbling block was the cost. Each of Kurt's new artificial testicles would, at the time, have cost Brian about £150, on top of which would be the cost of putting them in and monitoring their acceptance.

The vet, when I spoke to him, was happy to perform the surgery but a mite reluctant to commit himself to examining the dominant and non-anaesthetised Kurt's scrotum thereafter! But, faced with a bill approaching £500 for the whole job, Brian decided that his image could best be maintained with a new leather jacket at half the price and so simply forked out the £50 to have Kurt castrated and decided to tell anyone who asked either that Kurt's testicles had gone back into his abdomen or that he now owned a bitch. And if anyone was stupid enough to care, they'd probably believe either of those explanations. So everyone was happy and Kurt did indeed thereafter become much safer for Brian and the public in general to be near.

EIN, ZWEI . . . DREI, VIER, GOTT IN HIMMEL!

If Brian Smith's Kurt was the source of much consideration over the nature of a dog's physical appearance, at least the dog had only to fill the human demands of being a macho-looking dog. In the world of show dogs, much more is at stake with prizes, rosettes and accompanying esteem for the owner and perhaps the prospect of financial gain to be made by breeding from the winning dogs. It can often be a world where the welfare of the dog runs a distant second to the search for inferred glory by the owner and where the dog's suitability as a pet counts for little so long as it will stand still long enough and walk confidently for the judge. But the show dog must also be in good health, of course, and meet certain physical standards. Many of these standards are quantifiable and pertinent to the breed in question, such as desired height at the shoulder, while others concern more conjectural qualities such as 'should have a deep brisket' and are for the judge to decide. My opinions of the whole scene have oft been printed elsewhere, but basically, if owner and dog enjoy the performance, then fine. But if the dog doesn't enjoy it or the owner becomes obsessed and lugs the dog around the country, instead of giving it a happy and stable life as a pet, then I start to feel very sorry for the owner and even more sorry for the poor dog. Some people become totally obsessed about showing their dog and will do anything to try and improve their chances of winning, including booking themselves in at my clinics with a dog that has no behavioural problems other than a reluctance to be shown.

But visiting a pet shrink is nothing compared with the lengths that one Belgian owner went to. Owning what he believed to be an absolutely prime specimen of a Dobermann, he was dismayed to find that its testicles had failed to descend, a definite fault for an adult dog in the eyes of any judge. So, secretly he arranged for two implants, like the ones Kurt the Rottweiler's owner had decided against, to be inserted by the vet. He waited for the scars to heal and duly drove his dog across to one of the most prestigious dog shows in Germany. He felt that winning was a certainty now with a beautiful example of the breed with all tackle complete as the far as the judge would know. But disaster struck in the days immediately prior to the show. Amazingly un-noticed by the owner, the dog's natural testicles finally descended into the scrotum to join the artificial ones. As the dog came under the scrutiny of the judge, great confusion was caused. After all, dog judges need only to count up to two in that area and here was a dog with more, four to be precise! The man's guilt at interfering with the sexual appearance of his dog was, of course, laid bare and both he and the dog were duly disqualified. Whether he then had the decency to go back to the vet and have the artificial testicles taken out again, I don't know, but if ever one needed an example of just how much ridiculousness the sexual side of a dog could cause in human society then this is surely the case to beat them all. The dog, of course, was just a hapless victim of people gone stark staring mad in pursuit of recognition in their own manufactured world.

However, such people are little to do with normal humanity or the human/pet relationship as most of us enjoy it. And even though some pet owners seem to get very mixed up about the whole matter, the justifications for man playing god with the sex lives of our pet dogs and cats are now fairly clear. We live in an age when we increasingly need easily managed, well-behaved and non-aggressive pets and interference with their sexual reproduction and behaviour are almost unavoidable if we are to prevent disappointment in the relationship we demand. As a pet behaviour counsellor, thus far in this book I have naturally concentrated on the sexual behaviour of our pets and the effects of sterilisation on it, as well as the way that the sex lives of our pets affect our relationship with them. But just in case the purist in me that enjoys watching animals being entirely natural has given the idea that I am in any way opposed to the neutering of pets, it is only fair of me to now summarise the benefits and

drawbacks, including the medical influences, of that intervention and to point out that the benefits of sterilisation to the pet, its animal companions and passing contacts, and to its owners, their families, friends and passing contacts and to human society in general far outweigh the drawbacks. Despite owning a herd of neutered cats and dogs, I must also confess that I do somewhat lament the fact that most of our pets have to be surgically altered as a standard procedure to make it easy for them to share life in the human den, but accept that few people have the time, understanding, facilities or willingness to accommodate any sexual function or behaviour in their pets.

I must also say that I always chuckle when I hear that breeders have attempted to achieve lasting changes to their pets' sexual behaviour via the 'cure-all' of castration of a male dog or cat that was allowed to mature sexually and fully to be used as a stud. Having not produced satisfactory offspring or having simply been replaced by a younger fitter model, they, or the would-be owner that the poor creature was passed on to (or, unscrupulously to my mind, sold) as a pet, are so surprised to find that their castrated tom still sprays and tries to mount other cats and fights with other males, or that the stud dog persists in being what is now seen as a randy so-and-so with every bitch he meets in his new-found freedom. Their learned behaviour patterns are still fully active and probably always will be. More fool us for thinking that we could simply switch them on and off at will when we've had enough of managing their sexual encounters for our own benefit. The effects on behaviour that are possible to achieve in cats and dogs through castration are, as we have seen, usually age-dependent even if the animal is reproductively sterile after the surgery.

While I'm at it, I should also confess to long resisting my wife's calls to have Scud, my Border Collie cross

English Bull Terrier (yes, really . . . and boy, is he ugly!) castrated on the grounds of lack of any real reason for it in his behaviour. Just because as an adolescent many months ago he once cocked his leg over a bunch of flowers received from an admirer and placed lovingly in front of the fireplace is no grounds for such drastic action now that he's a fully adult and non-problematic male dog. In fact, I'm rather proud of his effort in passing comment against the good-looking swine who had the cheek to send the flowers to her, and wished I'd had the courage and lack of social grace to do it myself! But then, of the two sexes of our two major social pets, cats and dogs, male dogs are least likely to be neutered as a standard procedure anyway. If Scud were a bitch, he would have been spayed long ago, of course, to make absolutely sure that 'she' never reproduced her delightfully ugly self. Or is it just that I'd be next in the firing line if Scud were castrated? Therein lies the problem. It's so much harder to get it all in perspective when it's your own dog, of course, and that's why so many wives and husbands disagree so markedly when it comes to having the dog, if not the cat, castrated. The wife, perhaps conscious of the threat her husband may perceive, will often not make the decision without referring to her husband, yet will happily give the go-ahead for a bitch to be spayed at the veterinary clinic without consultation. When my clients have been faced with the prospect of having their male dog castrated, I've never yet had the husband take the suggestion without reacting. Usually it's a straightforward 'ouch', but the body language that accompanies it is more indicative of the threat felt. The man invariably crosses his legs tight and hunches up while his wife often forgets about the dog for a moment and looks on sympathetically at her husband, even though she may be laughing and far more relaxed about what may happen to their dog. But, as human reactions are so very important in the whole subject, here are the tables of what is likely to happen after the appropriate surgery for dogs and cats of either sex for all those couples or single owners who may still be wrestling with the idea.

Neutering

SPAYING QUEENS VIA OVARIOHYSTERECTOMY

Benefits

Prevents pregnancy.
Prevents problem of keeping noisy calling cats indoors during oestrus.
Prevents indoor urine spraying by queens in oestrus (in those that do).
Prevents attracting toms and having them loitering outside the house, spraying pungent urine and fighting noisily (especially at night).
Prevent false pregnancy in queens (rare).
Prevents ovarian problems, e.g. cysts and tumours later in life.
Reduces likelihood of pyometra (womb infection) – the susceptibility to pyometra increases in older queens, as the hormone cycles dilate the uterus facilitating contamination with bacteria.

Drawbacks

Risk of weight gain due to appetite increase. (Needs attention to diet.)
Minor risks of surgery – anaesthetic and infection.

SPAYING BITCHES VIA OVARIOHYSTERECTOMY

Benefits

Prevents pregnancy.
Prevents problems of not being able to walk dogs during oestrus.
Prevents 'mess' of bleeding around the house during oestrus.
Prevents attracting male dogs and having them loitering around the house with associated frequent urine marking.

Prevent false pregnancy.
Prevents ovarian problems, e.g. cysts, tumours and failure to cycle later in life.
Reduces risk of mammary cancer later if performed in young bitches.
Reduces likelihood of pyometra (womb infection). The susceptibility to pyometra increases in older bitches because the hormone cycles dilate the uterus and facilitate contamination with bacteria.

Drawbacks

Risk of weight gain due to appetite increase. (Needs attention to diet and exercise.)
Minor risks of surgery – anaesthetic and infection.
Possible link with incontinence, mainly in giant breeds.
Coat of feathered breeds such as the Afghan Hound and some spaniels may become woolly afterwards.
Some bitches urine mark more frequently after surgery (via lifting a leg to facilitate aim when squatting, though not total 'cocking').
Dominance aggression towards family members may be more marked after spaying of bitches that were already aggressive prior to surgery. (A problem highlighted in research carried out by my behaviourist colleague Dr Valerie O'Farrell at the Royal Dick (yes, really!) Veterinary School in Edinburgh.)

CASTRATION OF TOM CATS

Benefits

Infertility.
Reduction in inter-male aggression (though castrated toms may fall victim to entire males and suffer subsequent infection of wounds).
Reduced frequency of spraying.
Marked reduction in pungency of urine spray.
Reduced territorial roaming (thus increased time spent in and around the home).
Reduced likelihood or cure of 'stud tail' (blocking of active scent glands on tail).

Drawbacks

Minor risks of surgery — anaesthetic and infection (although less than with spay).

Potential physical appearance altered (due to failure to develop full secondary sexual physical appearance, e.g. 'full' face and scruff, when carried out on young toms).

CASTRATION OF MALE DOGS

Benefits

Infertility.

Reduction or cure of inter-male and human-directed dominance aggression leading to more compliant dog.

Reduction or loss of hormone-inspired sexual behaviour (dependent on age ofdog).

Reduction or cure of 'lovesick' dogs (whining, urine marking, becoming irritable or depressed and losing appetite and weight on catching scent of nearby bitch on heat).

Reduction in frequency or cure of indoor territorial urine marking.

Reduction or cure of escapology and roaming.

Reduction or cure of green, scented secretions from prepuce.

Drawbacks

Minor risks of surgery — anaesthetic and infection (although less than with spay).

Risk of weight gain without attention to diet.

7
Pet Perverts

'The craving to risk death is our last great peversion'
JOHN FOWLES

Most sexual behaviour in pets, or even what we sometimes erroneously misinterpret as sexual behaviour, usually has a logical explanation as I have tried to elucidate thus far in this book. But despite the best of caring intentions, we sometimes place our pets under extraordinary stresses. This is not only in terms of a severely altered social lifestyle but also, even when the appropriate hormones have been removed, in causing frustrations of the most fundamental kind. Social problems at integrating into the human pack are much more likely to be encountered by the dog than the cat, and sexual problems are also perhaps less likely in the feline because sex is a more functional affair and less tied up with social implications. Our standard policy of early sterilisation for tom cats also reduces the risk of aberrant sexual behaviour compared with their canine counterparts. But when the social or sexual frustrations get too much to bear for some individual pets, or certain exciting signals find their way into their brains, we can find that some of their responses and reactions may defy any logical explanation. The causes may be comprehensible, the treatment may be clear but the behaviour can reach depths of perversion that would demand a very long prison sentence if the perpetrator were human. This final chapter takes a look at some of the most remarkable cases of sexual deviance in pets that have passed through my clinic doors over the years. Some are weird, some are sad and some are just downright hilarious. In some cases, the difficulty wasn't the one I was being asked to treat, it was just an aside that the owners didn't find a problem with but which nonetheless was cleared up by the treatment for, say, over-attachment or dominance in their dog. But while some of the cases that follow responded well to treatment, some didn't and continue to defy known science. Take the case of Morris, for example.

BONKERS ABOUT CONKERS

Morris' owner called me in a state of desperation. Her cat, she said, was getting some sort of high from the plastic bag full of conkers that her two young boys and their friends had spent the afternoon collecting to have conker fights with later. 'Morris is simply standing there, a bit tense, with his nose right up close to the conkers through the hole he's ripped in the bag. He's got this concentrated look all over his face and seems to be grinning lasciviously over the conkers . . . it looks disgusting . . . his whiskers are twitching and he's stepping up and down with his back legs, I honestly think that he thinks that the conkers are a female cat. I can't seem to distract him and if I pull him away, he goes straight back. Is he okay, is this a normal thing for a neutered male cat to do with a bag of conkers or do I own a pervert puss? Help!'

Well, normalish . . . except that most cats don't get their kicks on bags of conkers, so we can presume that

Morris has his wires crossed somewhere, or perhaps has lost his marbles a little. It's all to do with chemistry. Like dogs, cattle and horses, cats possess a sense that is midway between smell and taste which allows them to concentrate smells in a special structure known as the vomero-nasal or Jacobson's organ, found above the palate in the roof of the mouth. To direct the scent-laden air over this half-inch long organ, the cat grimaces in a bizarre-looking manner known as a 'flehmen' reaction with its neck stretched forward and its top lip curled up in a snarl. The cat may appear to be in a trance with its ears slightly flattened and nose wrinkled as air is drawn in through the mouth in a series of short gasps while the tongue flicks back and forth over the two small openings to the vomeronasal organ behind the front teeth to dissolve the scent and direct it in.

However, the flehmen response is seen mostly as a reaction to scent left by other cats at spray posts or on faeces, rather than in cats 'scent-tasting' the smell of prey on the wind, though receptors in this organ do connect to areas of the brain concerned with the initiation of aggression and appetite as well as sexual responses. Flehmen is performed mainly by male cats and is particularly marked when they investigate the rear end of a queen in season or encounter her urine 'messages'. It has been found, like so many other 'male' reactions, to develop in response to the presence of testosterone, though it continues less frequently as a learned response in neutered males like Morris.

The vomeronasal organ is little understood because we do not possess it and though non-functioning vestiges of it can be identified in man, we can only guess at what the information it obtains means to the cat. We can only presume that Morris, a cat who lived his life permanently indoors by choice because he didn't like going outside, was misinterpreting the signals he was receiving from the conkers. Perhaps fresh-picked conkers give off some organic scent that is indeed similar to the scent of a queen on heat, though I have never encountered such a reaction in a cat before or since. Whether, without the intervention of his worried owner, Morris would have gone on to become a real conker bonker is probably doubtful, but what his owner saw when the lusty side of Morris came crashing into her kitchen was enough for her to get on the phone straightaway to find out what had happened to him. The fact that he was castrated didn't, as Russell Jones the cartoonist suggested, give him an unnatural interest in other nuts! As with the scent of a queen on heat, even a castrated tom is likely to 'flehmen' and get excited when he encounters the scent of her urine or something that to the deep seat of the reproductive side of his mind smells similar!

So strong is the drive to reproduce that it often remains even after we pet owners have surgically removed the prospect of it occurring in our cats and dogs. Finding a mate and mating itself are complex social procedures for we mammals, and not simply governed by the hormones that organise our sexual development and responses. While for the most part castration stops the development of the sexual secondary characteristics of their pet, and stops him doing 'blokish' things, often the effectiveness of the surgery depends on the timing. Castrating young males before they reach puberty stops the problems before they start, but once, like Morris, they've matured a little and tasted life as a true tom, castration may not stop the habits so well because they've become learned parts of his behavioural repertoire. But then there's still the problem of finding a mate, and the prospect of encountering a fertile queen, let alone one on heat, may range from slim in suburbia where all the other cats have been sterilised, to nil for the city cat kept permanently indoors. The chances of mating remain at nil, even if the waft or call of a queen in oestrus does percolate up through the window from the alleys below. Then we are dealing with a male cat, castrated or not, being sent all the right triggers, but one who is frustrated from doing what Mother Nature intended him to. And then the redirection of male sexual energy starts to happen, and sometimes in the most bizarre manner. Henry the Black Labrador cross seemed to lack access to the appropriate moment in a bitch's cycle and so found cycles of his own to play with.

BIKE SEX

Dear Mr Neville

We have regretted the day we bought our son a new bike for his birthday. His bright red racing bike has become an irresistible object of desire for Henry, our four-year-old Black Labrador. The bike is parked at night in our front hallway for security and Henry spends the evening trying to mount it from the front wheel angle or the rear. Come the morning or at any time when our son tries to take the bike out of the door, Henry must think that his lover is walking out on him because he tries desperately to mount it again and keep it in. More than once, son, bike and dog have ended up in an unholy heap by the front door. What on earth is going through our dog's mind?

Yours sincerely

Lesley and Alastair Grange

When the Grange family contacted me with this bizarre description of somewhat perverted canine excess, I detected more than a little mirth at their end of the phone. Not sure as to whether I was being sent up or not, I responded in jovial vein asking about Henry's normal sexual preferences. For instance, was he a rubber freak who simply found the tyres of the bike so attractive or was it really the whole thing, chain, lamps, drop handlebars, pump and all that had stolen his heart? Had he been so smitten with their son's previous bike, or with those of any of his friends? No, this was an entirely new and totally unexpected passion from Henry. The key change was that this new bike was now brought into the house at night, while the earlier less valuable models lived outside in the garage with the car. It was this that told me that Henry wasn't a sexual deviant of the mechanical kind, but simply a dog who perceived his status in the family as being under threat from metal competition. The fact that the bike was so lovingly cared for and even brought in to share the family den at night aroused what in human terms would be described as a large dose of jealousy in Henry, used to being the only dog in the home. But in canine terms, the new bike was a juvenile dog that had been afforded all sorts of privileges as soon as it arrived and the only way to deal with it was to make sure that it understood that its place in the Grange pack was right at the bottom and well under Henry! If it moved, or had the effrontery to attract attention or be taken out for a walk and a play from a higher member of the pack, the Grange's son, the dog was quick to attempt to put it back in its place. Not being a dog that had ever been seen to use any form of aggression in the form of teeth, Henry was employing the next most emphatic form of gesture on the new bike, dominance mounting, though there seemed to be some confusion about which end to dominate at the time I went to see the case.

Henry was clearly one very upset and confused dog and having explained the problem to the Grange family, we agreed that the best way to take the perversion out of their dog was to invest in two good solid padlocks, one for the bike itself and one for the garage door so that the bike could be safely stored out of the house at night and ridden off by their son without Henry being able to interfere. This they did, and the problem cycled away. In time Henry got used to the bike as he tended only to encounter it as a non-threatening pack member with its owner during walks and games in the local park and so maintained his position as 'best dog' in the family. As they were all the rage at the time, I just couldn't resist the temptation to quip that perhaps Henry was just confused about what type of bike it was that the son had been given. Not so much a racing model, perhaps more of a mountin' bike!

HOOVERING SEX

Dear Mr Neville

Our English Bull Terrier, Winston, has fallen in love with our vacuum cleaner. Every time I try to hoover the carpets I first have to put Winston in the garden otherwise he leaps on the poor machine and mounts it furiously. It used only to occur when I switched it on, but now he only has to catch sight of it and he's on it in a flash, humping like a dog possessed and with a strength of grip that is impossible to break loose. Poor Winston must think my vacuum cleaner is a bitch . . . how can I persuade him to think again?

Yours sincerely

Mrs Caroline Parker

This is, of course, a rather similar case to that of Henry. Poor Winston wasn't really a confused lovelorn dog, nor was he a demon sex pervert with a fetish about vacuum cleaners, though even I had to agree that Mrs Parker's model was a rather attractive shade of avocado green. Winston wasn't sexually motivated at all in his assaults, he was simply trying to keep this thing in its place, this thing that first had the cheek to deserve physical contact with the stroking hands of his owner, and then the sheer gall to hum and purr with excitement as the two danced around the floor together in front of his very eyes. Poor Winston. And Mrs Parker was right. Once he got a hold of his mechanical competition, he wasn't about to relinquish his grip and, as everyone knows, bull terriers of any type can be enormously strong. As I felt that it was a bit unfair to banish Winston to the garden, the outer reaches of his pack's den, whenever the hoover came out, we agreed instead on a two-fold approach to managing the situation. Ideally he would be taken for a walk while the carpets were hoovered but if this were not possible, Winston would be held on a lead and fussed and stuffed with his favourite titbits by another member of the family to show him that everyone else still loved him even if his mum had run off with that damnedly good-looking machine for a moment. And when the thing was finally put back in its cupboard, Winston could be there to see it rejected and then fussed and played with by Caroline to show that it was just a passing fancy. Winston seemed to be happier with this arrangement though I did get a call sometime afterwards to say that he had gone on the offensive and was now lying doggedly in front of the cupboard, and refused to budge whenever anyone tried to open it. He'd also had a purple fit when he'd heard a hoover in a television movie one evening and dashed to the cupboard and growled at the occupant, telling it to stay where it was or risk the carnal consequences. Wisely, the Parker's hoover decided to stay firmly put!

THE TEDDY BEAR'S MINE!

Dear Mr Neville

As we are a fairly quiet family I would admit that perhaps life isn't particularly exciting for our cat, Sweep, or our mongrel dog, Blogs, but then, as they are both castrated, we'd assumed that neither would be that interested in sex. We were wrong. It seems that not only is sex rampant in our house among the pets, but some degree of competition has crept in between Sweep and Blogs, who otherwise have always been the best of friends. But now both of this depraved pair seem to have developed a rather unnatural relationship with Rupert, my wife's teddy bear, and one she has owned and lovingly cared for since she was a child. We've caught both of our perverted pets mounting poor Rupert on several occasions and had to rescue the poor bear, but now it seems that he's caught in the middle of a strange love triangle. If either beast gets hold of him, the other tries to muscle in and take him away for his own purposes. Many's the time we've heard a series of low growls coming from upstairs and gone up to find them glowering at each other and swearing, with Rupert lying ravished on the floor in the middle. The more active and provocative Blogs has now taken to parading poor Rupert around the house in his mouth, teasing poor Sweep, though at such times the cat seems rather untroubled compared with his bad temper at others. How can we put our neutered pets' lives back in neutral and reduce all this tension?

Yours sincerely

Steven and Debbie McIntyre

The simple answer, as one might expect in this bizarre case, and one well worthy of the best tabloid newspaper, was that Rupert should be put away in a cupboard or kept in a room to which neither pet had access, and this was what was done and the problem soon went away. But Mr McIntyre had called me more out of curiosity over his pets' behaviour than in search of the obvious cure. A little delving into the history of the problem revealed that it had been Sweep who had first found comfort in Rupert's arms, but initially only platonically, as he had curled up asleep on the same soft chair in the McIntyres' bedroom. Perhaps he had accidentally knocked Rupert to the floor one day as he stood up but at this, or some other juncture, Blogs had seized the poor bear and begun to nuzzle him, and toss him around the room in play. As his excitement rose, fuelled doubtless by the scent of his owner and his friend Sweep on poor Rupert, the previously asexual Blogs began to mount Rupert at almost any opportunity. Rupert was rescued and Blogs chastised on several occasions but not before the rampant dog had presumably deposited some kind of sex-related pheromones on the bear. These in turn had, in some peculiar fashion, served to excite Sweep the next time he jumped up onto the chair for a snooze. Instead of sleep he too found himself unable to resist a quick passionate encounter with the now much abused and increasingly tattered Rupert. The whole thing had then spiralled up, or down, depending on your viewpoint. 'Sweep became the most disgusting, degenerate creature and would bonk Rupert any time he could wrap his legs around him. He grunted, groaned and then loudly chortled in ecstasy . . . and it happened every day, lucky little devil, until Blogs got even more involved,' said Steven in enthusiastic detail.

The more Sweep mounted Rupert the more Blogs became interested in the scent of the bear and the more the bear became a focus for their interest. Being a member of a more socially competitive species, Blogs then took to parading his possession of Rupert as a symbol of his status to Sweep, or anyone else in his pack who happened to be around. But if Sweep got there first and Blogs had to snatch his lover from that horrible feline blaggard, the two suitors fell out and growled at each other in an effort to frighten the opposition away. All of which is perfectly feasible given the evidence before us, but I'm pleased to say that now that the irresistible bear has been incarcerated for his own safety in Debbie's bedside cupboard, Blogs the dog and Sweep the cat are the best of friends again and the sexual beast within them both has gone on permanent leave. Unlike the more enduring case of Ching the Siamese cat and her unrequited passion for her canine friend . . .

YOU SEXY DOG, YOU

Dear Mr Neville

My cat's behaviour isn't really a problem as such but nonetheless my account is of an event that occurs several times a day. Both animals involved have pedigrees as long as your arm, with a liberal sprinkling of champions therein. Since she was spayed last spring, Ching, our chocolate-point Siamese cat, has developed what I can only describe as a seeming sexual fixation for Rolf, my eight-year-old male German Shepherd Dog. With tail erect and quivering, purring loudly, she flaunts her rear end right under his nose, two or three times per day. Poor Rolf's reaction is seemingly one of acute embarrassment. The flaunting display proceeds until I call a halt by hissing at Ching or clapping my hands to startle her or until Rolf slopes off to a quieter area of the house. This happens during the day . . . how she pesters the old fellow at night is a matter for guesswork. Ching's displays also startle some of our visitors; but there are among those some to whom a display of nature, if that's what it is, will do no harm. I did try discussing the problem with the receptionist at my local veterinary surgery but it took me some time to explain that it was a serious call and not just the teasing of a dirty old man. Even then, she couldn't offer much explanation. Has this sort of thing come your way before? If so, can you explain to me what is going on in Ching's sensual little head?

Yours sincerely

John O'Neill

Ching's behaviour sounded somewhat excessive, though probably not abnormal. Indeed, as we have seen in earlier chapters, similar behaviour is commonly observed in all cats when friendly towards their own kind, their owners, or to other friendly animals such as dogs with whom they share the human den. Sexual receptiveness and sensual rubbing is all part of the friendship for a cat. For example, when being stroked down the back, they will arch their rear quarters, erect their tail and adopt a flirtatious temporary receptive mating position. This is particularly common with friendly female cats, spayed or not, especially in fertile queens when in season, of course, and especially in Siamese cats, though the quality of the pedigree of either dog or cat in this situation is of no consequence whatsoever. High breeding brings no high social graces to the deportment of our pets when it comes to sex! But of the salacious nature of some Siamese queens I can speak from personal experience of my own two, including the champion feline slut of all time, Flirty Bottom, who was so named for her sensual performances with her sister and her owners and their dogs even as a tiny kitten.

Of course we encourage this type of behaviour, and

cats naturally come to make rubbing and flirting gestures far more often towards other animals with which they have regular contact. The behaviour seems to have been triggered after spaying with Ching, most probably as a response to all the extra close attention and nursing after the surgery, and she has since learned to use such behaviour to secure attention from man or dog as required. In Ching's case, she had always spent a lot of time in Rolf's company but especially so during the few days of her convalescence when he used to wash and lick her and let her curl up next to him while her scar healed. From Rolf's point of view, their relations could have been expected to return to normal once Ching recovered and became more active again. But for Ching, their relationship had been forged in adversity and she would continue to croon to him even without her sexual hormone cycle. Greater love hath no cat for her dog! Her behaviour, though annoying and perhaps confusing for Rolf, was essentially harmless, and I advised John simply to carry on as he was, provided it remained at the same level, but to try to give Rolf plenty of cat-free breaks every day to enable him to take a well-earned rest from the attentions of his most ardent admirer. Tough on Rolf to be so loved, but not nearly as bad as what Helga had to endure from her feline companion . . .

TRANS-SPECIES SEX

Dear Mr Neville

I am extremely worried about Monty, my ginger cat, who seems to have been driven into a frenzy of late by the mere sight of Helga, my short-haired Dachshund bitch. They are both three years old and have got along fine ever since I took them both on. Monty has never shown any interest in Helga from a sexual point of view but now he tries to mount her on a regular basis, even though he is neutered. About one in three of his assaults are successful in that being a large strong cat, he is able bite Helga's neck and hold her down to mount her. His actions are usually short-lived but are tantamount to rape. Poor Helga seems too afraid to move once Monty has mounted her and simply endures his rough attentions until he falls off and she can make a run for it. My vet has checked his records and says that there was nothing abnormal observed at the time of Monty's castration in the sense of one testicle being retained, or any such problem which could result in him still thinking he is a full tom, so we are at a loss to explain his sexual fascination for Helga. Can you help?

Yours sincerely

Charles Ritchie

This is one of my all-time favourite cases, not least because I was able to witness Monty in full hot flight and observe the total and utter look of surprise all over Helga's face as she realised that she'd been got again and had to let her feline sex-maniac housemate have his evil way with her. Poor Helga, but poor Monty too. Here was a cat, unburdened through castration of the need to be an all-fighting, all-mating feline survival machine who had suddenly been motivated to become a sex-obsessed fiend, and not even with one of his own species. Worse, surely, from the jeering viewpoint of his rivals in the garden, was that Monty was a creature possessed about the cat's traditional enemy, a dog, and a sausage-shaped one at that. The case was clearly serious and needed to be resolved for everyone's sanity, and fortunately I was able to hit the nail on the head as soon as I saw Monty in action. The problem lay not with his sexual preferences being fired up by an irresistibly attractive dog, nor from any testosterone surge as he was, quite clearly, a mature neutered tom. The problem lay within Helga's reproductive system. She had not been spayed but Monty had never shown any interest in her of a sexual nature even when she was on heat. This indicated that something may be amiss and sure enough, Helga's vet located a large ovarian cyst when I suggested that he take a look at her, rather than at Monty. Helga was duly spayed without delay and Monty's interest in her disappeared immediately. He never again tried to mount her and one must therefore presume that his previous attraction was triggered entirely by some unusual pheromone being given off as a result of her strangely active diseased ovary. In fact, Charles and I agreed that we should thank Monty for drawing his attention to Helga's condition as his reactions enabled the vet to intervene quickly and cure her before the disease progressed. It had been a remarkable and unique case for me, but the look on Helga's face as the maniacal Monty mounted her will live with me for ever. And if I never see another case like it, I will always thank Helga for showing me that emotional expression on a

dog's face can include surprise, resignation, confusion, indignation, hopelessness and fear all at once!

IS OUR CAT A HOMOSEXUAL?

'Are you my alternative?'

FLORYNCE KENNEDY (to a male heckler who asked if she was a lesbian)

Dear Mr Neville

We recently tried to introduce another cat to our home to give our existing cat, who is a four-year-old neutered male, a playmate because we are away at work all day and thought he might appreciate some company. We went to the local cat rescue shelter and found a beautiful black neutered male aged between one and two years. But when we brought him home and showed him to Biggles, our existing cat, all hell broke loose. Biggles was not impressed at all, but then again, perhaps he was. After hissing and glaring at Sooty, as we called him, Biggles then leapt after him and proceeded to mount him furiously. It didn't look very loving or friendly and frightened Sooty so much that we thought it wiser to take him back to the shelter straightaway, but now we are worried about Biggles. Is he a frustrated homosexual cat or was this just a strange one-off reaction?

Yours sincerely

Nicola and Tony Trenbath

I must first apologise for including the question of homosexuality in the perversions chapter, but in animal terms, there is nowhere else for this issue to be addressed. While apparently homosexual relations are commonly observed in the more social animals, as we have seen, what we infer as sexual behaviour is, in fact, usually a form of social interaction other than sexual. Dogs, rabbits and cows of the same sex may mount each other in an effort to resolve conflicts or define their relations in terms of social order, and it is interesting to note that animals with a more solitary lifestyle, such as the hedgehog, have never been recorded as demonstrating homosexual behaviour nor homosexual-type social displays. Cats, though they are often social with their own kind, as solitary hunters have no need of very much definition in their social order with their fellows, unlike the pack-living dog, and so their language and communication patterns are rather different and less well developed. Not only do cats apparently demonstrate a narrower range of facial expressions than dogs but they also tend not to resolve conflicts with mounting displays, preferring instead to use staring encounters and the options of attack or retreat. Only in very rare and highly-charged circumstances such as Biggles' have I ever encountered a pet cat mounting another in an effort to dominate and control it, and this has usually concerned the reaction of an established castrated adult pet male cat to the arrival of a new cat or kitten in his home. The resident, who usually has never been known to have any friendly contacts with other cats at all, simply boils over when confronted with another cat of any sex or age in his living room and reacts with a range of highly aroused behaviour. Usually there is an out-and-out attack on the hapless new arrival as well as staring and lots of hissing and spitting at every meeting. This is best diffused by the new arrival by remaining absolutely still but, if they make a run for it, the movement will often ignite the rage of the resident who will immediately give chase. If he catches up, and can corner or grab the new cat, he may then pin him or her to the ground with the neck grasp used by male cats when mating, and proceed to mount the new cat very roughly. And all the owners wanted was to get another cat to double their fun and give their original cat some feline company! My job as a behaviour therapist then is to try to help the two cats get to know each other in a more controlled and safe manner (see my earlier book, *Do Cats Need Shrinks?*) or decide whether introducing any other cat to the house can be successful or worthwhile from anyone's point of view. But for sure, feline mounting in this type of situation is very much the product of an emotional overload and, as it can be directed towards either sex of cat by either sex of cat, neutered or not, can hardly be described as homosexual mounting.

THE GAY ROTTWEILER

Dear Mr Neville

I own a very large and very strong, tough-looking male Rottweiler. He is well trained, well behaved, a good guard and is no problem to anyone. He loves me, he loves my family, including our two young children, and he happily accepts our friends into the home once we have welcomed them. So where lies the trouble with Arnie? Well, we think that he is a homosexual dog. Not that that worries us particularly, but his sexual preferences are tending to get him into trouble with other male dogs in the park who really don't look upon his approaches as he would seem to hope they might! He shows no interest whatsoever in bitches, instead preferring to chase every male dog he can find. He's been attacked for his cheek in trying to mount a couple of dogs but thankfully has not retaliated, what with all the worries about nasty Rottweilers at the moment. I'm sure he isn't cut out to be a fighter but being told 'No' in no uncertain terms by other male dogs doesn't seem to have taught him any lessons. Do we really have a gay dog and, if so, how can we manage the likely repercussions on his lifestyle and social contacts?

Yours sincerely

Gavin Terry

Mutual grooming, licking and close physical contact are observed commonly between friendly dogs of all sexes, especially those in a cohesive pack, whether wild or in the human den, as any owner of a small pack of pets can testify. Such physical contact is all part of maintaining relations in the same way as we humans touch members of our family and close friends far, far more than those unfamiliar to us. For less familiar human contacts of either sex, we have ritual and non-threatening forms of touch such as a handshake at greeting, while hugging and kissing is more common between the sexes as friendships develop. Dogs in a pack, or even two strange dogs meeting, are generally far more tactile than we humans. Vocal communication accompanying physical gestures indicates how people are feeling, but dogs tend to be rather quiet with each other by comparison, relying more on body posture, eye contact, scent and body contact to convey their moods and social reactions. In a pack environment, actual sex is restricted to a male and female, usually a single breeding pair, even though close physical contacts and sexual posturing are vital forms of communication within the group. While experimental sexual mounting may occur between individuals of the same sex in adolescent gangs of males or females, this cannot be interpreted as forming the basis of an emotional relationship, merely as practice for each individual to develop his courting and mating ability with a member of the opposite sex when or if the opportunity presents itself.

Sex for the dog, cat or any other animal is, after all, the means whereby they and their genes reproduce themselves, so genuine lengthy homosexual relationships between adult dogs serve no function whatsoever and would be likely to disrupt pack stability if they did occur. In any case, one must question the depth of any breeding pair relationship in the pack. Its function is to provide the best opportunity for the pack to raise young and, while there is no doubt that the fittest male and female spend much time together and will usually pair for life, the nature of the sex between them is perfunctory and designed to allow the dog to deposit his sperm in the bitch when she is at the right stage of her cycle for her eggs to be fertilised. Sexual fulfilment, if that is the word in the animal kingdom, is solely the premise of the male, who reaches orgasm and usually quickly, in order to ejaculate. There is no need for bitches, or any female of any other species, to have an orgasm during mating in order to ensure successful reproduction, and so they don't. An alternative of a homosexual relationship between two females is therefore of little or no benefit in a sexual sense and so long as sexually and socially fit breeding males in a dog pack have access to females, they will attempt to mate simply in response to the scent cues they encounter from the bitches.

However, this is the situation in a balanced and stable dog pack. The vast majority of pet dogs do not live in such a social order. Yet their hormones run through their system, motivating them to search for mates and ensuring that they respond to the appropriate cues, if, say, the scent of a bitch wafts to them on the wind. But this is without any of the social rules that would govern their responses or even limit their physiological ability to react if they were in a pack situation. The result can be that misinterpretation of the signals they do receive can be common and hyper-excitement in the face of any form of sexual or social opportunity can lead them to proposition any dog of any sex, or even the cat or their human owners at home. Or, as we have seen throughout this book, a male dog's sexual energies can be directed or diverted onto bizarre and inanimate objects such as teddy bears and blankets. But while such obsessions and homosexual liaisons can develop in male pet dogs, they seem to me to be a function of their restricted lifestyle and lack of social opportunity to meet a range of dogs and bitches. Given increased opportunities, perhaps even simply by the acquisition of a companion dog of the opposite sex, the obsessive or homosexual tendencies usually disappear, even though the new bitch may be spayed and no concrete pair bond ever develops between them. Their previous behaviour was more a function of social isolation than sexual frustration or a homosexual character.

Apparently homosexual relations are commonly observed in social species kept in zoos, due largely to the effects of lack of environmental, intellectual and social stimulation and while, in human terms, to call such homosexual relationships a vice is rather less than liberal minded, this is indeed the case with animals in such circumstances. Given a broadening of their environmental, social and intellectual perspective and opportunities, the level of vices, homosexuality, and indeed, levels of other instabilities, decline dramatically. In psychological experiments, overcrowding in laboratory rat populations has also been shown markedly to affect the level of homosexual mounting in both sexes, though again this is more a function of frustrating social conditions and simply one of a range of responses to the instability in the group. But then, aggression levels and vices such as stereotypic pacing, circling and weaving, and self-mutilation also occur . . . in fact, the instability, loss of intrinsic social regulation and expression of bizarre behaviour patterns all rather mimic what happens to the psychology of people in over-crowded cities when stress levels rise.

TEMPORARILY DUCKING THE ISSUE . . .

I have also seen what in ill-considered human terms might be described as homosexual relations developing between my two drakes, Hissing Sid, a large and extremely ugly Muscovy Duck, and Cherry, a slighter and fast moving Indian Runner cross. Originally they were part of a flock of four, two ducks and two drakes and everyone got along, the boys mounted the girls throughout the breeding season and they produced lots of very mixed parentage eggs. The fact that we ate them all was no deterrent to what Mother Nature ordained for them. But then sadly, and within a couple of weeks of each other, the two girl ducks died and Hissing Sid and Cherry had only each other for company. Through the winter, they were fine together but with the arrival of spring, a young duck's fancies turn, as ever, to thoughts of raising a family. But, in the absence of any girls, the two boys simply did what their hormones instructed them to by mounting the next best thing available . . . each other.

Ducks, like cats, are not particularly gentle when it comes to sex and very soon poor Cherry had a large feather-less patch on the back of his head and neck and even the much larger Sid was looking a bit thin in the same area where Cherry had managed an occasional successful leap. But even though the two of them bonked away very frequently and went through the entire mating performance as if they were each with a lady duck, their homosexuality was hardly occurring through choice. Rather than keep a pair of semi-bald, or semi-oven-ready ducks around the place, we soon went out and got another seven ducks, two more drakes and five females. And now, as one would expect, Hissing Sid and Cherry have lost all interest in pursuing and mating with each other and happily chase their harem around as nature intended.

But what of Arnie the Rottweiler who is apparently given plenty of social and mental stimulation and who meets plenty of bitches of all shapes and sizes in the local parks? Surely his preference for members of his own sex amounts to homosexuality when he so clearly finds bitches of no interest whatsoever? A little detective work into his upbringing revealed the cause of his attitude. Arnie had been one of an all-male litter of four Rottweilers which had been removed from their mother at weaning and kept together in a large separate room. Unfortunately, their breeder had then found it difficult to find good homes for them all due to recent adverse publicity about the breed following some rather unpleasant incidents up and down the United Kingdom at the time. As a result, although one was placed at about four months of age, Arnie was the last to go at eight months old, having spent all his formative weeks solely in the company of other young males. Because of this, he just didn't know what to do with bitches or how to do it and only the scent or sight of a male dog held any interest for him in terms of social encounter.

As he went into adolescence, his own testosterone was indeed making him more sexually aware and responsive, but only building on the social cues and opportunities presented by his familiarity with other males. Arnie was, in fact, conditioned to be a homosexual dog by the simple fact that his breeder never appreciated how important it was for him to meet a whole range of other dogs and bitches, having left him with his brothers and concentrated on trying to ensure that all of them were very good with people. In fact, given this sort of sheltered upbringing, they were very lucky that more serious behavioural problems didn't result. It's this type of lack of attention to wide and proper socialisation of puppies that produces many of the nervous, socially incompetent and aggressive dogs that get referred to me for treatment.

In terms of 'treatment' for Arnie, it was a case of trying to make up for lost opportunity. The stern rebuffs of unwilling male dogs were no more than occupational hazards for him and our only hope was to increase his interest in and social abilities with bitches rather than isolating him from other males. To this end, Mr Terry acquired a two-year-old Dobermann bitch called Sheba, already spayed, of course, to prevent the advent of any 'Rotterman' puppies once Arnie had learned to be heterosexual. Initially Arnie showed no interest in his lively companion but, before long, her playful insistence awakened memories of the relationship he had had with the only other bitch he had ever known, his mum. Soon he began to lie next to her with his head on her flank and then began to play with her. Before two weeks were out, they were the best of friends and Arnie was starting to experiment with her a little, though receiving the customary rebukes for attempting to sniff her rear end too closely. Being good-natured, Sheba simply ran away when Arnie tried to mount her rather than snapping at him, which might otherwise have confused him for a while longer, and so he learned very quickly how to relate to and court the other bitches that he met. As his abilities improved, his interest in his own gender waned from a sexual point of view, though he continued, as any dog should, to be sociable and keen to interact with other males. Arnie is now a socially well-balanced dog and his remarkable case demonstrated just how elastic the social and, by implication, the sexual nature of dogs can be. More important even than that was that Arnie's behaviour showed just how closely linked social ability and learning opportunity are to a dog's sexual expression and competence.

Homosexuality as humans interpret it is then something of a misnomer in the animal kingdom, though certain gestures, confusions, conflicts and developmental restrictions may cause some individuals of the more social species to give us the impression that they are homosexual. But homosexuality is counterproductive in a world where there is little or no emotional aspect to sex and certainly it is of no benefit in the procreation of the species. On these bases alone homosexuality can probably be said not to exist, not even among the higher apes closely related to our species.

On the other hand, our pets certainly do demonstrate some very odd sexual activities which are similar to human obsessions and sexual symbolism. Many of their vices are traceable to the fact that their lifestyle with us precludes reasonable opportunity for many of them to develop normally in a sexual sense. Such a lifestyle may force them, through lack of social contact with their own kind, to focus their sexuality onto us, or our toys and furnishings, but most such apparent pet perverts are nothing of the kind. They are quite simply, in human terms, frustrated and responding to the social, environmental and hormonal circumstances that they find themselves in. But while we can detach ourselves emotionally relatively easily from the dog or cat that mounts the teddy bear or the dog that appears to be homosexual, the behaviour of others can all get a bit close to home sometimes. Take the case of Hamish, for example.

KNICKERS!

Dear Mr Neville

We have something of a depraved Cairn Terrier called Hamish. He is quite a stroppy little so-and-so, can be quite possessive over his toys and bones and often tries it on with the lady dogs he meets in the local park. But, for the most part, we enjoy his pushy stubborn little nature and try to avoid conflict when he wants his own way by letting him have it. But one thing that he's always done is really very annoying, and that has now progressed to the point where we feel we really ought to treat it, is that he will empty the dirty linen basket whenever he gets the chance. This used to be as far it went, but then he started to guard the clothes and wouldn't let us near them. So we walked away and left him to it, and sure enough he would eventually leave them and come downstairs to make friends with us again. But now he has started to mount our dirty clothes, especially our underwear, and becomes extremely aggressive if we try to push him off or take it from under him. We didn't mind him stealing it, or even guarding it . . . but mounting it and then trying to bite us if we come near is all a bit too much! All suggestions for help gratefully received.

Yours sincerely (and running out of clean underwear)

Barbara and Leonard North

There are many dogs in all parts of the world which develop a fascination for the contents of the dirty linen basket. To us, it's a fairly depraved activity but for the dog, maintained in a human pack where scent communication with his pack is non-existent, our soiled clothes represent an oasis in a barren world. Underwear especially contains similar scents and sexual pheromones to those that are key factors in the mechanisms of communication between dog and dog. So even though our interest in such scent is negligible at the conscious level (though perhaps far stronger in our subconscious than we realise with regard to what attracts one person to another), it's not surprising that our pet dogs should take such interest in our discarded clothes. A casual initial interest in a playful puppy is, of course, often compounded by our reactions in trying to rescue our dirty linen and prevent the little blighter from running downstairs to parade our underwear in front of all and sundry. The puppy soon learns how to get our attention and though the behaviour may switch to clean clothes, towels from the bathroom, ironing and dishcloths, the dirty washing is always the caviar of the range because of the scent. Naturally, the scent itself can trigger canine sexual interest in our dirty linen in male dogs, especially at the adolescent phase and especially in dogs fired up with lots of testosterone and/or deprived of access to their own species. It's a resource well worth guarding if you can get possession of it and tuck it well underneath you to make recovery difficult. That's if you're trophy-conscious and perceive yourself to be quite dominant in your human pack. The best way of dealing with this, as Hamish's owners did, is to reduce the importance of the trophy by ignoring the invitation to enter a conflict that can't be won and walk away, while ensuring that the dog is then denied access to the dirty linen or kept out of the bedroom altogether. But many of us want the dog in the bedroom or actually aren't sharp enough to remember to keep a persistent little dog out, least of all first thing in the morning when we're trying to dash to work. And for many dogs, the comfort of a sweaty unwashed old shirt to lie on can make all the difference to feeling secure when their owners are away from home and is something oft recommended for dogs who suffer from separation anxiety. (Common symptoms of this condition are barking and howling, destructiveness, and loss of toilet control. Treatment suggestions are outlined in my previous book, *Do Dogs Need Shrinks?*.) It's also quite fun really to play

chase games with the dog if he cheekily steals your clothes or towel. But having him mount them is a different matter!

Barbara and Leonard quite understandably decided to call a halt to their tolerance of Hamish's interest in the contents of their linen basket, but if a possessive dog guarding a trophy is tough enough to deal with when you simply must have your property back, a dog who is engaged in pursuit of sexual pleasures with it is even harder to shift. Sexual arousal will switch all too quickly to aggressive defence if dogs like Hamish are threatened at such times. At this point, it is still essential to avoid conflict and to try to distract the dog by ringing the doorbell or rattling the food bowl or biscuit tin downstairs. Reward the dog for complying and then put him in a secure room or outside so that he can't enter the race and beat you back up the stairs to the object of his desire. Then you really have to make sure that he can't get at the linen basket by keeping him out of the bedroom or putting the basket in the bathroom and keeping him out of that. Most importantly, resolve immediately to take a careful look at his hormonally-inspired behaviour relative to his age and provide more opportunity for him to socialise with other dogs. A little reward-based training in responding to the request 'leave' may also help, but while the offer of a favourite titbit may encourage him to relinquish possession of a tea towel or clean shirt grabbed in play, it's unlikely to provide sufficient motivation to give up his pheromone-packed silky knickers sexual partner. But then would you be persuaded to stop having sex if someone offered you your favourite chocolate bar? Food may run sex a close second for many, but for Mao the Siamese cat, the two went firmly hand in hand . . .

SAFE SEX WITH A CONDOM-EATING CAT

Dear Mr Neville

Mao is my Siamese neutered male cat. He's always had a bizarre fixation about eating wool and occasionally used to eat rubber bands as well, though thus far it has all passed through him without causing any harm. Some months ago, Mao discovered the joy of eating condoms and taught himself to steal them, one at a time, from the packet by my bed, open the little foil sachet and disappear off to some quiet place to consume his prize. Most times he didn't actually eat them, but he did chew them for ages, and of course render them absolutely useless! My girlfriend and I thought this was a huge joke but having come home to find that Mao had either dragged each one out of its packet to chew it or just chewed holes through the foil in all the condoms in the packet, we embarked on a sustained effort to put them in places that he couldn't find or reach. The bedside table drawer presented no problems to Mao, as he soon learnt to open it and then he taught himself how to open the wardrobe and retrieve his favourite snack from the shelves or even from the jacket pocket where I had concealed them. Eventually the bathroom cabinet, secured behind a closed door, proved too much even for the resourceful Mao and he restricted his rubber obsession to the occasional rubber band. Some weeks passed and we had almost forgotten about Mao's predilections, until last night. The best way to explain what happened is to say that we were about to make love and the condom had just been fitted to the appropriate part of my anatomy in order to fulfil its intended purpose when Mao struck. From nowhere, but most likely from under the bedside table, he leapt onto the bed, grabbed me and sank his teeth into the condom . . . and me! I can assure you that this was about the most painful thing I have ever suffered and probably about the funniest thing my girlfriend has ever seen. As I write, the tears are still rolling down her face, as they did down mine, though for different reasons, and neither of us can really bring ourselves to make love again so long as Mao is in the room. I've heard of many forms of bizarre foreplay, but getting on your hands and knees to make sure the cat isn't in the room must be one of the most unusual and least erotic in the whole history of mankind. Is there any other way of curing Mao's rubber fetish?

Yours, scarred emotionally and physically,

Robert Tiffin

Mao, sent packing immediately after his dreadful lunge, was one of many Siamese and Burmese cats especially that have strange dietary fixations. This seems to be an inherited disorder and triggered in some between weaning and about two years of age by some form of stress, such as being homed too early as kittens or moving house. Most cases concern wool and other fabric eating but many of those also eat rubber.

Pica, as this ingestion of non-nutritional items is known, was the subject of an extensive research project that Dr John Bradshaw, his colleagues at Southampton University and myself carried out in 1990–91. Though our investigations demonstrated that the problem is far more widespread in the Siamese and Burmese cat populations than we had first thought and gave many useful pointers to the origins of the problem, we came up with few new ideas either for treatment or for problem prevention, other than for breeders of these types not to use known sufferers for breeding.

Descriptions of the origins of the problem and treatments which can be partially or even sometimes totally successful, can be found in *Do Cats Need Shrinks?* but, needless to say, Mao is a unique case of a wool-eating, rubber-eating cat that has developed such an unusual depraved eating disorder. More accurately as far as Robert and his girlfriend are concerned, I should say that Mao 'was' a unique case because although the emotional and physical scars of the first incident healed soon enough, Mao managed to secrete himself successfully on three more occasions and make his excruciating pounces. The pair of them soon became thoroughly fed up with his obsession.

They also, quite understandably, got fed up with the lack of spontaneity in their love-life which had become restricted to the bedroom and only after an often prolonged and worried search and chase of the cat. Robert phoned to cancel his appointment to bring Mao to my behaviour clinic, so alas, I never actually got to meet this remarkable oriental pussycat.

Instead, Mao had been taken to the local cat rescue shelter to be found another home, with the bizarre instruction to the staff to enquire as to the method of contraception used by any potential new owners. When such a strange proviso to adoption was explained, it probably caused many cat-seekers to forget taking on a high-born pedigree cat and move quickly on to the moggies, so beware! The shelter people may have grown tired of watching the interest of potential owners for Mao evaporate and now don't ask, hoping that he won't behave in such a way in his next home. Mao may still be there in his rubber and fabric-free pen, just waiting for a new owner . . . like you!

VICTOR THE VOYEUR

Dear Mr Neville

We own what must be the world's most disgusting Maine Coon cat. Victor is, quite simply, a voyeur and, if he were human, would surely be one of the 'dirty mac' perverts that skulks around people's homes trying to catch a glimpse of them without any clothes on. Whenever my wife and I are getting undressed to go to bed, or come out of the shower, there is Victor, leering at us. And, if ever he gets the chance to be in the room when we're making love, he sits there staring at us, wide-eyed and transfixed. It really became so off-putting that we had to banish him from the bedroom and started to keep a water pistol handy in the bathroom to shoo him away with when his voyeurism got too much. He was castrated years ago and shows no interest in his own kind, and is normally an affectionate cat who purrs and enjoys a cuddle and a stroke when he wants one without getting at all turned on. He has never actually tried to approach us when we're naked . . . he just sits there gawping at us and enjoying the show. We've taken to keeping him out of the bedroom, at least, but the little blighter is getting clever at hiding himself away if he can get in during the early evening, for example. He comes out later after we've gone to bed, appearing on the top of one of the wardrobes or silently nestling himself so that only his head pokes out between the closed curtains. Now we've started to develop a sixth sense about being watched and usually know when the 'pussy pervert', as we call him, is about, but we're also starting to imagine that he's there when he's not! Paranoia has set in because of this wretched cat . . . is there anything we can do to encourage him in healthier pursuits?

Yours sincerely

Lt Col (rtd) and Mrs Gerald Browning-Smith

While Mao's oral rubber 'perversion' almost certainly had its roots in some genetic abnormality, there is no doubt that sex between owners can be enormously interesting to their pets. As well as watching their people behave in such a unique way relative to their normal countenance and the

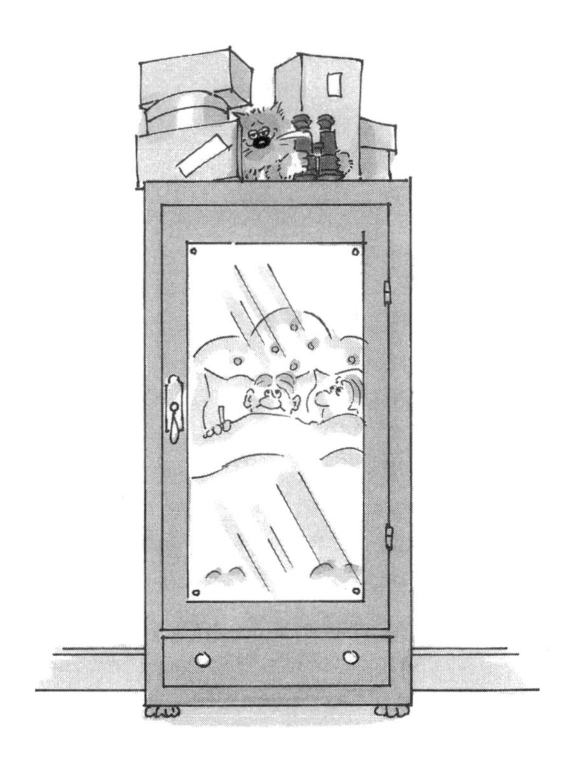

attractions of social excitement generated at such times, we may tend to forget the effects that the scents being given off by our increasingly sexually aroused bodies is also very likely to be of irresistible fascination to cats and dogs. For the vast majority of their lives we ignore all their scent signals, make no direct use of any of our own smells to communicate with them and deliberately and frequently wash our body scent away, covering what remains with clothes and then masking or replacing it to appeal to our own kind with perfume and after-shave. And then bang! Off with the clothes, out with the sexual organs and associated pheromone-laden natural lubricants, turn on the sweat and away we go. No wonder that even the neutered dog and cat can often look so confused and sometimes want to be part of the action that nature always programmed them to respond to but which their owners had kept hidden from them all this time. Victor the Maine Coon cat is a very common, but far less harmful example than Mao of what can happen when our pets are around when their owners are laid bare from the scent point of view or are simply trying to get on with their sex-lives. In true army fashion befitting the military nature of his owners, I suggested a change in routine for Victor to encourage him to take up healthier feline outdoor pursuits of hunting and territorial defence during the evening and at night by locking the cat flap, unless the Browning-Smiths were ready for him to be part of the family. However I stopped short of suggesting frequent cold showers or the electro-convulsive therapy that the good Colonel had felt might be an appropriate way to deal with his pet pervert. Lord knows what he might have suggested for Shah the Persian cat who was a lot more active in his owners' sex life. . .

SEX 'N' VIOLENCE OF THE FELINE KIND

Dear Mr Neville

Last night I brought Paul, my new boyfriend, home for the first time. Everything was fine, we enjoyed a great meal, watched a really slushy film and then went to bed, feeling very warm and passionate. But as we were mid-way through a splendid steamy love-making session, Shah my Persian cat leapt onto Paul's upwardly pointing backside and sank his teeth into him. Paul, as you can guess, leapt up in mortal pain, whereupon Shah proceeded to attack him repeatedly with his paws and teeth. It took the both of us to suppress Shah and we had to wrap him in a blanket to get him under control. We threw him in the living room and closed the door and when I went back later to see how he was, he was back to his normal fluffy friendly self. Poor Paul was really quite badly scratched and scarred but, thankfully, doesn't seem to have been put off by the incident. Why did Shah react like this, he's never been anything other than friendly with all my friends and family? Did he get out of control through jealously or did he think that Paul was attacking me and try to defend me (we were being quite noisy!). We'll be keeping Shah out of the way in future but do you think I am at any risk living with this cat of mine? Is he likely to attack me out of the blue at some other time in future or do you think he might have some violent psychological disorder that you might be able to treat?

Yours hopefully

Amanda Green

Amanda and Paul must have thought that things were really going well until the moment that Shah decided that he could no longer control himself. I suspect that his attack was a painful case of redirected excitement caused by the behaviour of his owner and her new boyfriend and especially in response to the unusual noises and particular smells that they had invaded his home with. All this served to excite him, probably even sexually, as we have seen can be possible even in a castrated cat, though he would not have known what to do with his new-found feelings. His emotions simply overloaded into the next nearest form of sudden expression: aggression. That he attacked Paul was almost certainly unrelated to any feelings of jealousy or desires to protect his owner from being ravished. Shah attacked Paul probably because his backside was a moving target at the centre of all the activity and, cats, as we know, are programmed as predators to chase moving targets readily, and rapidly bobbing ones even more readily. Once aroused and in attack-mode, some effort on the part of Amanda and Paul would indeed have been needed to restrain poor Shah, and he would have continued to lash out once confronted by a justifiably upset Paul.

But Shah's reactions, though unusual, were by no means abnormal in their expression and, like most severely upset or excited cats, he calmed down quickly once removed from the situation. His reactions were indeed specific to the circumstances that he was presented with and Amanda was no more likely to be attacked by her cat at any other time than before this unfortunate incident. The treatment I suggested, as with the case of Victor, was based on keeping the cat out of the bedroom when Amanda and Paul were furthering the physical nature of their relationship and to encourage him to spend more time outdoors in the hope that he would find excitement of a more fitting kind. Like many of the treatment suggestions

I offer to my clients, that was easier said than done and required much effort on Amanda's and Paul's part as they were a young couple who probably didn't have the time or inclination to think for too long about where the cat was on their frequent visits to the land of passion. Indeed, they had clearly only just managed to get themselves out of the Shah-less bedroom in time, clothes askew, when I rang Amanda's doorbell to keep my appointment. And that was one reason why I didn't feel professionally inadequate about nearly dying with laughter when, as Amanda told me the story, Paul dropped his trousers to show me the huge weals, scratches and bite marks on his backside!

Of course, in such cases it is all too easy to assume that the cat is indeed feeling jealous about what his owner's friend is being allowed in terms of physical contact, even though the cat obviously never gets into such a position himself. Feline reactions to sex are rarely likely to concern anything that even vaguely resembles jealousy and can nearly always be explained totally to the owner by other means, however obscure.

With dogs, however, matters are slightly more confused because they are pack animals and relationships between a dog and its owner-packmates and their human friends are, in its mind, all important to its survival and to its relative status. As a result, most family owners can describe some level of reaction in their dog when they kiss and cuddle, or play physical games together or argue and fight. All such interactions between the humans have some bearing on the dog's position, his or her own relationships with the people involved, and feelings of security for the pack as a whole. It is probably the case that most dog owners around the world who allow their dogs to share their home will find that their dog wants to be part of the scene whenever they are in prolonged or close physical contact. Indeed one survey found that 65 per cent of dogs tried to nuzzle or push their way in between their owner couple if they were enjoying a kiss or a cuddle and the figure would be higher if the close contact concerned a familiar owner and a friend who wasn't a permanent part of the group. The dog's reactions may be even more pronounced during squabbles. Some dogs try to get in the middle to separate the couple, others stand some distance away and bark, both to signal they're upset that their pack may be disintegrating and to try and get the couples' attention onto them and off the problem in question. Yet more leap to the aid of their favoured half of the arguing pair and attack the other, presumably the choice being the one that the dog feels most closely pair-bonded to within the pack or who represents most strength if the pack is to divide. They do not necessarily help the one who feeds and walks them. That said, it is often the lady of the house who gets defended and the man who then feels rounded on and doubly hurt by the whole problem.

The dog's reactions may be thoroughly understandable if it feels it is being left out of affectionate pack socialising. After all, dogs or wolves in packs maintain their social cohesion partially through mutual rubbing and weaving together to exchange individual scents and develop a communal scent that contains elements of each member of the group. So if the 'breeding' pair openly start to get physical, the dog may feel he has every right to join in to ensure that his scent is included. In families where the dog's position is unclear, vulnerable or artificially high, rivalry for access to an individual may also be the motivating factor for it to try and get between a cuddling or warring couple. Such situations probably occur at some time or another with just about all dogs that live as house-pets. Possessiveness and subsequent protection of one particular member of the family from all others can also result because a young dog sees that individual as part of its 'gang' or even the other half of its pair bond on which its own position in the group depends. Other particularly high-ranking individuals may actually feel that as top dogs, they alone are the ones who have the right to initiate the pack's mutual rubbing ceremonies and therefore try to break up the efforts of any others, especially if they look like they might lead to mating. But all this, though thoroughly interesting to myself and all other students of the human/pet relationship, is as nothing compared with the ultimate incursion of the dog into our lives.

AN UNHOLY THREESOME: MAN, WOMAN AND MAN'S BEST FRIEND

Dear Mr Neville

This is an extremely embarrassing letter to have to write but I would appreciate some advice about what to do with Roger, my wife's large Weimaraner male dog who insists on taking part in our love-making. The problem began when he reached about a year and a half in age (he is now nearly two) and decided to leap out of his basket in the corner of our bedroom, onto the bed and onto my back while I was making love to my wife. He clasped my waist strongly and proceeded to thrust at me violently, fortunately with an extremely poor aim, and then had the cheek to snarl at me when I clobbered him off and sent him back to his bed. He didn't learn any lessons from his first mistake and kept attempting a repeat performance over the next weeks, so much so that I tied him to his basket when putting him to bed at night. Unable to get to us, he started to bark and howl, which is a most effective form of birth control, I can tell you! Naturally, I took his bed out of the bedroom after this and put it next to the radiator in the kitchen where I thought he might be comfortable. No such luck. He howled and whined so much that we couldn't get any sleep, let alone make love, so now he's back in the bedroom and we've settled for a truncated love life and a decent night's sleep. I don't want to upset the dog or make him feel unloved in any way, but our sex-life has been, as you might put it, 'Rogered' by bad luck. Do you have any last ideas to help us . . . before I consider shooting the dirty mutt and risk divorce anyway?

Yours sincerely desperately

John Fischer

The explanations for Roger's perverted behaviour lie in the preceding pages of this book and the reactions of his owners at the time I went to see them lie in the Book of Tolerance. But Roger's fate ultimately lay in my helping Mr and Mrs Fischer get their dog's life in their human den into some sort of perspective. And if ever a pair of owners needed a motivating force to achieve that aim, sex, or the prospect of the lack of it, was the deciding human factor. Under this type of assault on their sensibilities, the Fischers came to realise far quicker and more assuredly than most just how confused their poor dog must have been in his relations with them, his pack, and in the restrictions of a sexual kind placed on him simply by virtue of his being a family pet. Inside all our dogs beats the heart of a social wolf craving for definition in our den. In their hormones and in their deep, instinctive patterns of behaviour, they obey the divine commands of their genes, irrespective of our efforts to manipulate their minds and train their actions. In their sexual responses, our cats and dogs react instinctively, and often in spite of what we do with their sexual organs or cycles, 'rough hew them how we may'.

For Roger, the price of life as a pet was to have his position in the Fischer pack made clear . . . at the bottom, in fact so far down that the thought of mounting his owners would be seen as a serious social challenge. Then he received a shot of anti-male hormone treatment and, gradually rather than suddenly, found his basket moved towards the bedroom door, out into the hallway and finally down the stairs to the kitchen. While all this was going on he was introduced to lots of other dogs, and walked especially with a local bitch that he'd taken a shine to. It all took some time for John and his wife to apply and it wasn't easy for them to come to terms with having to move Roger out of the bedroom and behave consistently as higher-ranking dogs towards him, rather than giving off confusing signals that gave him the impression that he could join in their fun. But, as John said to me some weeks after I had called to see them, and by then well able to acknowledge his anthropomorphism, 'It was either that or I would have had to fake an orgasm every time he jumped on me!' Roger and Mr and Mrs Fischer are all well, sexually defined and living happily in the south of England.

'He prayeth well, who loveth well both man and bird and beast'
SAMUEL TAYLOR COLERIDGE